CRAFT
BEER
REVOLUTION

JOE WIEBE

CRAFT BEER REVOLUTION

THE

INSIDER'S GUIDE *to* B.C. BREWERIES

DOUGLAS & McINTYRE

Douglas and McIntyre (2013) Ltd.
PO Box 219, Madeira Park
British Columbia, Canada VON 2HO
www.douglas-mcintyre.com

Edited by Caroline Skelton
Cover and interior design by Jessica Sullivan
Maps by Eric Leinberger
Index by Stephen Ullstrom
Printed and bound in Canada

Douglas and McIntyre (2013) Ltd. acknowledges financial
support from the Government of Canada through the
Canada Book Fund and the Canada Council for the Arts,
and from the Province of British Columbia through the
BC Arts Council and the Book Publishing Tax Credit.

Cataloguing data available from Library and Archives Canada

ISBN 978-1-77100-115-1 (pbk.)
ISBN 978-1-77162-001-7 (ebook)

Allison—

What a long, strange trip this has been. It may have taken longer than either of us bargained for, but I'm so lucky to have had you at my side along the way. I look forward to many more adventures with you in years to come.

Love, Joe.

CONTENTS

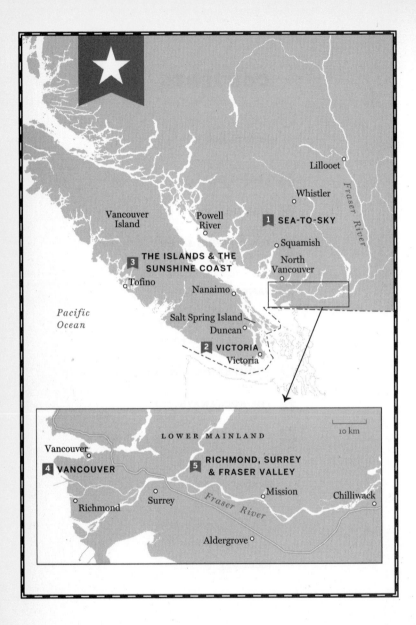

1 SEA-TO-SKY

3 THE ISLANDS & THE SUNSHINE COAST

2 VICTORIA

4 VANCOUVER

5 RICHMOND, SURREY & FRASER VALLEY

Lillooet

Whistler

Vancouver Island

Powell River

Squamish

North Vancouver

Fraser River

Tofino

Nanaimo

Salt Spring Island

Duncan

Victoria

Pacific Ocean

LOWER MAINLAND

10 km

Vancouver

Richmond

Surrey

Fraser River

Mission

Chilliwack

Aldergrove

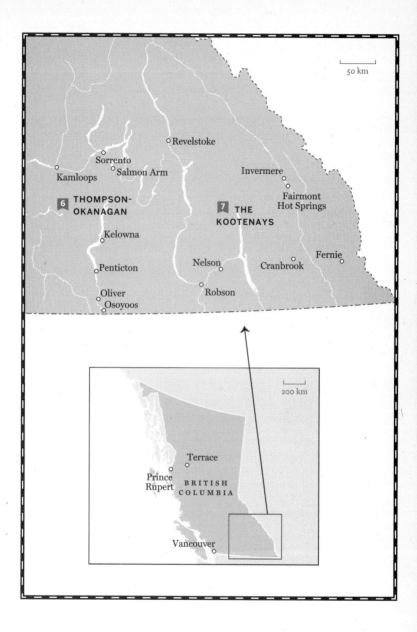

50 km

6 THOMPSON-OKANAGAN

7 THE KOOTENAYS

Revelstoke

Sorrento
Salmon Arm
Kamloops

Invermere
Fairmont
Hot Springs

Kelowna

Penticton

Nelson
Robson

Cranbrook
Fernie

Oliver
Osoyoos

200 km

Terrace

Prince
Rupert

BRITISH
COLUMBIA

Vancouver

INTRODUCTION

Welcome
to the Revolution

•••••••••••••••••••••••

BRITISH COLUMBIA'S craft beer revolution began thirty years ago in the unlikeliest of spots: the tiny village of Horseshoe Bay, half an hour northwest of Vancouver. It started back in 1982 when a couple of persistent—one might even say stubborn—beer lovers built a small-scale brewery using old dairy equipment and began brewing an English-style mild ale for the Troller Pub across the street.

Horseshoe Bay Brewery was Canada's first modern-day microbrewery. Its very creation went against the tide of the preceding seventy years. Until 1982, twentieth-century Canadian beer history was bleak: the Great War, Prohibition (yes, we did suffer from that malady, too, although not for as long as our American neighbours did), the Great Depression, and another world war squeezed much of the life out of the beer industry in Canada. In the post-war era, big breweries monopolized what was left, leaving consumers with almost no choice in what sort of beer they could drink: mainly it was yellow, fizzy and bland.

Although Horseshoe Bay Brewery only survived for a few years, by building it, Frank Appleton and John Mitchell started a revolution. Since then, Canada's brewing landscape has changed radically and irrevocably. Governments have reformed archaic liquor laws and brewing regulations, often because tenacious brewers pushed them to do so. Where once it was nearly impossible to get anything other than a nearly flavourless version of Pilsner beer, there are now so many styles of beer available that many craft beer lovers are arguing for a return to simpler styles—like Pilsner.

The word "microbrewery" didn't even exist before 1982 but it has since become an everyday term that itself has undergone a revolution, or perhaps a rebranding, into "craft beer." From an economic standpoint, craft beer has grown from nothing into a significant player in the marketplace—December 2012 sales figures from the provincial liquor distribution branch indicate that as much as 17 per cent of the domestic beer sold in B.C. comes from small- and medium-sized breweries—more than $150 million annually. And the craft beer market here has been growing at a pace most hedge fund managers would drool over: expanding by more than 25 per cent each year with total sales more than doubling over the past four years. This during a so-called economic downturn.

The first twenty-five years of the microbrewing movement saw relatively steady growth. After Horseshoe Bay Brewing broke the ice in 1982, there was an initial burst in 1984 with the arrival of three more breweries that are still flourishing today: Spinnakers, Granville Island Brewing and Vancouver Island Brewery (originally named Island Pacific Brewing). New breweries arrived in waves over the next two decades—and there were many closures, too, as prospective brewers learned of the challenges associated with this brand-new industry.

And then everything exploded. In 2007 there were thirty-five breweries and brewpubs operating in B.C., but in the six years since then, another fifteen have opened, including seven in 2012 alone. As 2013 begins, there are fifty craft breweries and brewpubs in B.C. and by the end of the year, another eleven are expected to open, mostly in and around Vancouver.

The craft beer revolution has also spread beyond breweries and brewpubs to include restaurants and bars that are entirely focused on craft beer: so-called "taphouses" like the Alibi Room and St. Augustine's in Vancouver that have more than ninety taps between them exclusively serving craft beer from B.C., the Pacific Northwest and Europe. Restaurants host beer-pairing dinners and hire certified cicerones (the equivalent of a wine sommelier in the beer world). You can find cask-conditioned beer on tap any day of the week in Vancouver and Victoria, and cask events occur in other communities around the province all the time. Beer festivals take place—and sell out quickly—in Victoria, Penticton, Vancouver and the Koote-nays every year. Many private liquor stores showcase craft beer above and beyond anything else, and there are several specialty distributors devoted to sourcing difficult-to-find craft beers from around the world. And often the people buying these beers are not planning on drinking them any time soon; yes, cellaring can apply to craft beer as well.

B.C.'s craft beer revolution has been an exciting adventure over the past thirty years, but it's far from over. Vancouver has only recently awakened to craft beer, and now its near-insatia-ble thirst is leading to the birth of new breweries as well as big expansions for extant operations. Craft breweries across the province from Tofino to Fernie are drawn by Vancouver's gravi-tational pull—if they brew good beer and can get it there, it will sell. And that, precisely, is what the craft beer revolution has been about from the start: good beer, crafted by folks who care about beer first and foremost, enjoyed by people who crave an authentic, delicious product.

Welcome to B.C.'s craft beer revolution. If you don't know much about craft beer, you've come to the right place. This guidebook will get you started, and if you want to learn more, the community of beer lovers and brewers in British Columbia is very accessible and will happily welcome you into its fellow-ship. If you already consider yourself a hophead or a beer geek or just a plain old beer lover, then I hope you will learn something new in this book—perhaps an aspect of the history, an anecdote from a brewer, or even a beer you haven't tried yet.

Most of all, I hope this book will become dog-eared and beer-stained, its pages inked over with your own comments and tasting notes as you take it with you on the road to explore B.C.'s burgeoning beer scene. Cheers.

WHAT IS CRAFT BEER ANYWAY?

The term "craft beer" is a brilliant piece of rebranding that was undertaken collectively by the entire microbrewing movement in North America. I have asked many different people—brewers and writers—who have been involved in the industry for decades when they first heard the term used, and most people point to the mid- to late 1990s. Personally, I noticed it coming into vogue a little later than that, a few years after the turn of the millennium. Since then, it has expanded across North America and even beyond to the rest of the world.

This rebranding itself is a big part of the reason why craft beer has taken off in the way it has. Instead of "microbrewing" or "micro beer," which really just means small beer, the term "craft beer" carries much more meaning and value. By linking beer with the local food scene—something wineries thought to do a long time ago—craft brewers started to connect with vast new markets. The result has been a boon to the industry and a sustained boom in craft brewing.

The original term, "microbrewery," comes from government taxation law that divides the industry into groups based on their brewing capacity: for example, in Ontario, a microbrewery must brew less than 50,000 hectolitres per year (1 hectolitre, a commonly used measurement in brewing, is equal to 100 litres) in order to qualify for lower tax rates. Here in B.C., there is a three-tier system with micros coming in under 15,000 hL, a regional category that covers anything above that up to 150,000, and then everything else above that.

If you want a more specific definition, a craft brewery is a small-scale operation that produces less than 150,000 hL per year (or less than 1 million hL in the U.S.). The brewery must be independent, and it must be dedicated to brewing high-quality beer using only the best ingredients. Another harder-to-define criterion is the idea that craft brewers are in business to make good beer, not just to sell a whack of it. Of course, they have to sell beer to make money, but that should not be the sole intention. As Garrett Oliver, the brewmaster at Brooklyn Brewery, writes in the *Oxford Companion to Beer*, "craft brewing universally involves boldly flavored beers coupled with a defiantly independent spirit."

When it comes down to it, you know it when you taste it.

A B.C. CRAFT BEER ODYSSEY: PLAN YOUR OWN ADVENTURE

Over the course of two decades living in Victoria and Vancouver, I visited most of the craft breweries near those cities long before I started working on this book. As a freelance beer writer for newspapers and magazines, I travelled to many different communities to visit breweries for stories. And as I began writing this book, I set out to visit the remaining B.C. breweries I'd never been to before. In the end I managed to get to all but one—Plan B Brewing in Smithers, which closed up shop before this book went to press.

As research for this book, I undertook a big road trip around the bottom half of the province, what I called my Craft Beer Odyssey. I love driving, so the chance to drive across the province and back was a thrill for me, even if my schedule was jam-packed without much time to sightsee or spend more than a day in any one place. I drove 2,364 km in a clockwise loop from Vancouver up through Squamish to Lillooet, then across through Kamloops, Sorrento, Salmon Arm and Revelstoke, down to Invermere, Fairmont Hot Springs and Fernie, and then back east to Nelson, Robson and Osoyoos before returning home to Victoria. I spent eight days on the road, visited six breweries and three brewpubs, one winery, one hop farm and one craft beer–focused pub. I also went for one horseback ride (my first ever), relaxed in a hot spring, swam in a lake, and even took a ferry ride—the longest free ferry in North America, actually, which crosses Kootenay Lake just east of Nelson.

I found even more evidence of the strong growth of the craft beer industry in B.C. than I was hoping for—many of the places I visited are smaller, somewhat isolated communities, so I wasn't sure if the burgeoning success the industry is enjoying in Greater Vancouver, the central Okanagan and Vancouver Island would be reflected in those places as well. But I couldn't have been more wrong. Whether it was Kamloops, Revelstoke, Fernie or Nelson, the story was the same: local consumers are embracing craft beer like never before and the breweries are doing all they can just to keep up with demand.

I offer this as an example of the sort of beer-soaked adventure you could use this book to plan. My Craft Beer Odyssey was an incredible trip and I highly recommend you discover B.C. with your own similar adventure.

For help planning a B.C. vacation, go to www.hellobc.com.

THE THIRSTY WRITER

My own beer-soaked history began in Niagara-on-the-Lake, Ontario, in the mid-1980s when I wasn't old enough to drink the stuff legally. Surprise, surprise: most of my teenage beer drinking involved a Molson or Labatt product. But luckily there were a few influences in my young life that inspired my interest in what was then the brand-new microbrewing movement.

One was my older brother, Pete, who had developed an interest in British and German beers while travelling and working overseas. When he visited from Toronto we'd often go out to see a movie, including a pre-show pint or two at a British pub next to the movie theatre—although I was only seventeen or eighteen, I never seemed to get asked for ID when I was there with my older brother. I remember enjoying the richer flavours of Bass, Double Diamond and Smithwick's, and was proud to take my own friends there later when we were all of age.

Another influence was my friend Ken, who learned home brewing from his uncle. While still in high school, he actually arranged for a teacher to take him and a couple of his buddies, me included, on a field trip to a microbrewery—Wellington County Brewing in Guelph. This amazes me today since we were all underage, but the teacher must have seen the value of this for Ken. It certainly paid off since Ken went on to study brewing in Germany and has been a professional brewer for fifteen years.

Most craft beer aficionados have a "conversion moment," an event or episode in their life when they discovered craft beer and became hooked on it. Mine occurred on a backpacking trip to Europe with another buddy, Glen, in the spring of 1991 when Ken was studying in Germany. Glen and I landed in Frankfurt, found the train to Freiburg, and then walked with already-too-heavy packs to Ken's *Studentenwohnheim* (student residence). Ken took us to a pub and ordered three bottles of beer—something called Hefeweizen, which I'd never heard of back in Canada. Before he allowed us to taste it, however, he showed us the proper way to pour it. He carefully tilted the bottle so that the amber liquid flowed down the side of the tall, curvy glass. He stopped before the bottle was empty, leaving a couple of inches of beer in the bottom. Then he did something crazy: he turned the bottle on its side and rolled it back and forth on the top of the bar, stirring up the dregs at the bottom of the bottle. Finally, he poured the lees over the beer in the glass, leaving the cloudy yeast in suspension in the beer itself and a two-inch head of foam on top.

As interesting as this demonstration was, that wasn't my moment of epiphany. My first sip of the Hefeweizen was. I'd never seen or tasted anything like it before: yellowish-orange and cloudy with a thick, creamy head on top, effervescent almost like champagne, and with a fruity, banana, bubble-gum flavour. I loved it immediately. That moment transformed me forever—suddenly I didn't just want to drink beer, I wanted to sample it in all its different forms. It was a revelation.

And that's what Glen and I did over the next eight weeks, all over Europe and the UK, often forgoing proper meals so that we could try another pint of beer instead. I can still remember, even taste, so many of them. Black beer in a pub next to the Charles Bridge in Prague. Guinness at the seven-hundred-year-old Brazen Head Pub in Dublin. Creamy Austrian lager in litre steins in a Salzburg castle cellar. A nondescript lager in a train station somewhere in France—the half-pints were so expensive we decided the glasses they came in must be included in the price and stuffed them in our backpacks. I still have that glass. A long row of draught handles in a pub in Edinburgh with numbers for names (60/-, 70/-, 80/-), which we found out was traditionally based on the price in shillings of a hogshead of the beer in question—we tried them all. And on our final evening in London, pooling our few remaining coins for one last shared pint—we flew home from Heathrow the next morning with just a few pence in our pockets. My journal from that trip reads like a beer guidebook.

Sure, I liked beer before that trip, but the quality and variety of the beer I encountered all over Europe changed me into a beer lover on a different scale. The mass-market Canadian beer I returned to did not taste nearly as good. From then on, I sought out good beer wherever I went.

I moved to Victoria a few months after my trip to Europe, and now I've lived in B.C. for half my life, which I think qualifies me as a British Columbian. After arriving here, I began exploring B.C.'s nascent microbrewing scene in earnest. I loved discovering a new brewery or brewpub, and I have always been on the lookout for something new at the liquor store. But I didn't seriously think about being a beer writer until I was walking through California's Sonoma vineyards for a travel story for the *Vancouver Sun* in 2008. I was there with a dozen wine writers. On the second night, they staged an intervention of sorts: I guess they'd had enough of me talking about beer all the time, so they sat me down and told me that I should do what they did—except I should write about beer. It seems obvious now in retrospect, but it was as if a light went on in my head. From then on, while it hasn't been the only thing I write about, beer has increasingly become the focus of my stories. I branded myself as the Thirsty Writer and didn't look back.

The next step in that evolution is the book you are holding in your hands. Hopefully, it will benefit from the knowledge I have gleaned in my quest for beer over the past twenty-five years or so. Thanks for joining me on this journey. May your thirst, like mine, be unquenchable.

GLOSSARY OF TERMS

•••••••••••••••••••••••

THERE ARE a few acronyms and terms in this book with which
some readers may not be familiar. If you know them all already,
consider yourself a certified beer geek. Otherwise, here are
some definitions.

ABV

This stands for "alcohol by volume," the typical way alcohol in
beer is labelled. The most common beer styles (Pilsners, pale
ales, wheat beers, ESBs, etc.) generally average 5 per cent ABV,
while IPAs and many stronger Belgian styles may range from
6 to 8 per cent ABV. Heavier imperial porters, stouts, barley
or wheat wines and Belgian "quads" might top out over 10 per
cent ABV.

ale

In its current definition, ale refers to a class of beers made
using the top-fermenting yeast *Saccharomyces cerevisiae*, as
opposed to lagers that use a bottom-fermenting yeast. There
are dozens of styles of beer running the gamut of flavours
and descriptions that all might be considered ales, from pale
ales to porters, saisons to stouts, and *Hefeweizens* to Belgian
Abbey ales. The word ale came into the English language
from the Danish word *"öl."* Prior to the sixteenth century,

British brewers disdained the use of hops and referred to foreign brews that did use hops as "beer," calling their own version made without hops "ale."

bomber
This is the colloquial name for the 650 mL bottle, which has become the standard size for single bottle sales in the North American craft beer industry. Craft breweries usually put their core brands in six-packs and their more unusual seasonal or limited release beers in bombers.

CAMRA
The Campaign for Real Ale was founded in the UK in 1971 and in B.C. in 1985.

ESB
This stands for Extra Special Bitter, a popular British ale style that is also often referred to simply as "bitter."

growler
Growlers are 1.9-litre (half-gallon) refillable bottles that resemble mini moonshine jugs and can be refilled at many craft breweries and brewpubs in B.C.

Hefeweizen
A German wheat ale, usually cloudy with suspended yeast, that has an effervescent body and a fruity banana, bubble-gum aroma and flavour. Perfect on a summer patio.

hops
Hops are the flowers or cones of *Humulus lupus*, a climbing vine that grow vigorously up to 15 metres tall. There are dozens of different varieties of hops, which are divided generally into two groups: bittering and aroma. Bittering hops are added early in the brewing process, as the wort (unfermented beer) is boiled, while aroma hops are added towards the end of the boil. Adding aroma hops to the fermented beer later on is called "dry hopping," and this results in a highly aromatic and flavourful hop character.

IBU

This stands for "international bitterness units," which is a measurement of the saturation of the alpha acids derived from hops in beer. Although it is not officially a scale out of 100, there is a theoretical saturation limit of 110, and anything past 100 cannot really be discerned by the human palate.

IPA

India Pale Ale—originally an English ale style that was brewed for export to British subjects living in India, it became very popular in the late nineteenth century and then lost its appeal when Pilsner lagers gained international prominence. Craft brewers began reimagining the style in the 1980s and 1990s, using hops grown in the Pacific Northwest that exhibit extreme bitterness as well as potent pine and citrus flavours and aromas. It has since become the flagship craft beer style by which breweries are often compared.

lager

As with ale, lager is a generic term for a class of beers made using a bottom-fermenting yeast (*Saccharomyces pastorianus*), which is best fermented at cooler temperatures than ale yeasts. In a general sense, lagers are considered cleaner and crisper than ales because the yeast tends to ferment more completely and produce fewer fermentation byproducts. The word comes from the German verb *lagern*, which means "to store" because lagers take longer to ferment than ales and had to be "lagered" in cold caverns during the warm spring and summer months prior to mechanized refrigeration. Today, 90 per cent of the beer consumed in the world is lager, primarily the generic international Pilsner style brewed in mass quantities all around the world.

pilsner

What we now call Pilsner was originally an attempt by a Czech brewer in Plzen to re-create the brown lagers made in neighbouring Bavaria, but using Bohemian ingredients. The resulting happy accident was a new, golden lager with a sweet, malty body and an assertive floral, grassy hop character. The style caught on and eventually took the world by storm.

saison
The French word for "season," this Belgian "farmhouse ale" style is very dry, highly carbonated, and fruity (thanks to the Belgian yeast). It is usually bottle-conditioned (refermented in the bottle), which can result in a cloudy appearance and sediment in the bottle. It can range from 5 per cent to 8 per cent ABV with a hop bitterness range of 20–40 IBUs. Delicious and refreshing.

taphouse
These pubs with multiple taps (usually at least twenty, but often as many as forty or fifty) are ideal for craft beer lovers because of the variety they offer. Taphouses often sell sets of four sampler glasses, which give customers the opportunity to try different beers without having to buy a whole pint (or sleeve or glass) of each one.

wit/white ale
Cloudy and effervescent, this is the Belgian equivalent of a German *Hefeweizen*, but the Belgian yeast imparts more of a spicy character that is often enhanced by brewers adding bitter orange peel, coriander or other spices.

1

★ **SEA-TO-SKY** ★

AT THE BREWERY	DRAFT	FOOD	GROWLERS	BOTTLE SALES	TOURS	BEDS
BrewHouse High Mountain Brewery	✪	✪	✪			
Bridge Brewing			✪			
Howe Sound Brewing	✪	✪		✪		✪
Whistler Brewing	✪	✪	✪	✪	✪	

CRADLE
OF THE
REVOLUTION

....

I DECIDED to open this guidebook with the Sea-to-Sky region because it is home to the town of Horseshoe Bay, where the craft beer revolution began in 1982. Although Horseshoe Bay Brewery is no longer in existence, the region still represents a good starting point—for both the craft beer novice and the grizzled veteran who thinks he or she knows everything about beer already.

Sea-to-Sky refers to the highway that runs from North Vancouver up to Whistler. It's a rugged, winding route that is exhilarating to drive when it isn't bumper-to-bumper, but it can also be a dangerous road, especially in winter conditions. This is a region for all-season outdoor enthusiasts: you can hike, bike, climb, camp, dive, kayak, canoe, snowshoe, ski or board to your heart's content. And then when you've tired yourself out, you can relax with a great local beer.

The Sea-to-Sky region includes some of B.C.'s oldest breweries and one of the newest. Whistler Brewing dates back, in various ownership configurations, to 1989, and Howe Sound Brewing in Squamish was established in the mid-'90s. Squamish, the midway point between Vancouver and Whistler, was also home to the Tall Ship Ales company, a brewery that was greatly respected for its high quality and innovation—they brewed the first bottled India Pale Ale in B.C. that I am aware of. Sadly, that company didn't survive.

North and West Vancouver seem primed for a brewing explosion. Cut off from the main part of Vancouver by two very busy bridges, I expect that North Shore beer lovers would welcome a few breweries or brewpubs to call their own. Right now there is only Bridge Brewing, one of the newest breweries described in this book, but not long ago there were two brewpubs there too: Sailor Hagar's, where Central City's Gary Lohin came into his prime as a brewer, and Taylor's Crossing Brewpub (originally Avalon Brewing), which was part of the Mark James Group's chain of brewpubs, but unfortunately closed in 2011.

Plans are in the works for a new brewery in North Vancouver called Deep Cove Brewing. And wouldn't it be wonderful to see B.C.'s craft beer revolution come full circle with a new brewery in Horseshoe Bay? Maybe if we dream it, it will happen.

www.markjamesgroup.com/
brewhouse.html

604-905-2739
4355 Blackcomb Way, Whistler
E-MAIL brewhouse@shaw.ca

BrewHouse High Mountain Brewing Company

Tap List

5 RINGS IPA

7% ABV | 60 IBU

Go for gold with this Olympic-calibre IPA.

GRIZZLY BROWN ALE

5% ABV | 15 IBU

A rich and full-bodied English brown ale.

||||||||||||||||||||||||||||||||||||||||||||||||

THERE ARE LOTS of places where you can enjoy yourself after the ski hills close in Whistler Village, especially high-end restaurants that will satisfy wine lovers, such as the Bearfoot Bistro where you can personally sabre a bottle of champagne in their extremely well-appointed cellar or sample vodkas in an ice-encased room that hovers at −27°C (don't worry, they supply parkas). But when it comes to craft beer, there isn't much choice. The BrewHouse is about it.

The good news is that the beer is really good. The BrewHouse is part of the Mark James Group chain that includes Yaletown Brewing in Vancouver and Big Ridge Brewing in Surrey. Brewer Derrick Franche gained a lot of fans in the craft beer community when he was brewing at Dix in Vancouver back before it closed in 2010. While there are a couple of basic brews on the menu here, you can count on the Big Wolf Bitter and Grizzly Brown Ale. And be sure to try the 5 Rings IPA, the top IPA in the 2012 B.C. Beer Awards.

Facts & Figures

OPENED ‣ *1997* ✪ **STYLES PRODUCED** ‣ *5 + seasonals* ✪ **ON TAP** ‣ *The brewpub* ✪ **GROWLERS** ‣ *Yes*

Bridge Brewing

www.bridgebrewing.com
604-770-BREW (2739)
115-2433 Dollarton Highway
North Vancouver
E-MAIL info@bridgebrewing.com

||||||||||||||||||||||||||||||||||||||||||||

"**VANCOUVER'S FIRST NANOBREWERY**" is a welcome addition to the North Shore. Situated in a non-descript business park just east of the Ironworkers' Memorial Bridge, the small brewery is an attempt by founders Jason and Leigh Stratton to "break out of the corporate world and do something fun and exciting." After planning the new brewery for a couple of years, they invited elite chef Patrick Doré, with whom Leigh was working at the Fairmont Waterfront Hotel in downtown Vancouver, to join them "on the flavour side" as they began to set up the operation in early 2012.

Jason, an accountant by trade, applies dollars-and-cents pragmatism, saying he will "let the business dictate when we'll be able to hang up the shirt and tie" and leave his day job as a controller behind. For now, he and Patrick brew on evenings and weekends while Leigh brings in their baby (born just five days before Bridge's opening) to sell growlers to thirsty customers.

Tap List

NORTH SHORE PALE
5.6% ABV | 27 IBU

A tasty Northwest-style pale ale, well-balanced with a nice hop bite over top of a solid malt base.

DEEP COVE IPA (seasonal)
6% ABV | 56 IBU

Only available occasionally, this West Coast IPA is definitely worth braving the bridge traffic for.

Facts & Figures

OPENED ▸ *2012* ⚙ **STYLES PRODUCED** ▸ *1 + seasonals* ⚙ **WHERE TO BUY** ▸ *At the brewery or at the Edgemont Liquor Store* ⚙ **ON TAP** ▸ *A few restaurants and pubs in Vancouver area* ⚙ **GROWLERS** ▸ *Yes*

www.howesound.com
604-892-2603
37801 Cleveland Avenue
Squamish
E-MAIL hsibrew@howesound.com

Howe Sound Brewing

||||||||||||||||||||||||||||||||||||||||||

JUST AS THE sheer rock face of the granite monolith known as the Stawamus Chief towers above the town of Squamish, one hour north of Vancouver, Howe Sound Brewing stands out in the B.C. landscape of craft beers—at least their unique, one-litre "pot-stopper" bottles do.

When siblings David and Leslie Fenn opened this brewpub, restaurant and inn in 1996, they thought it would be a case of "If we build it, they will come," but Leslie acknowledges it was a tough go at first. "The tourism scene wasn't here yet," she admits. But these early adaptors persisted, and as tourists began discovering this mecca of outdoor activities (and Vancouverites began noticing the low cost of housing), Howe Sound Brewing was ready to serve beer to them all.

The Fenns conscripted B.C. brewing legend John Mitchell, who lives relatively nearby in North Vancouver, to help design the brewhouse. Mitchell also developed their original recipes and still keeps his hand in the mix, dropping by every Friday to poke his nose in and point out to Leslie and the brewing staff what they're doing wrong. I say this with complete affection for John, but it's absolutely true! (See "John Mitchell" on page 22.)

Tap List

BALDWIN & COOPER BEST BITTER
5.5% ABV | 52 IBU
John Mitchell's own recipe, this is a pitch-perfect ESB.

KING HEFFY IMPERIAL HEFEWEIZEN
7.7% ABV | 25 IBU
Like a picture of a solid German Hefeweizen seen with 3-D glasses, this beer explodes with flavour.

PUMPKINEATER IMPERIAL PUMPKIN ALE (seasonal)
8% ABV | 19 IBU
Howe Sound does imperial styles so well—here's another great example. Bursting with pumpkins and spices.

TOTAL ECLIPSE OF THE HOP IMPERIAL IPA (seasonal)
8% ABV | 90 IBU
An incredible beer—not for the faint of heart, but definitely for the hophead!

In 2001, provincial rules that had kept brewpubs from selling their beer off-premises were loosened, and Howe Sound responded quickly by making their beer available on draft throughout the Lower Mainland. They began bottling in their distinctive flip-top bottles in 2007, and grabbed attention among craft beer lovers with a wide range of offerings, surprising considering the limited size of their brewhouse. Thus far, Howe Sound has released twenty-eight different beers, including obscure styles (Berliner Weisse), political critiques (Bailout Bitter), and cheeky brands such as the Three Beavers Imperial Red Ale that skated close to Olympic trademark restrictions with a label that showed off gold, silver and bronze medals won at brewing competitions draped around the necks of ultra-Canadian beavers.

Brewmaster Franco Corno has built off of Mitchell's original recipes and applied his own personal touch, which often leans toward the "imperialization" or amplification of traditional styles, as he has done very successfully with the King Heffy Imperial Hefeweizen, Total Eclipse of the Hop Imperial IPA, Pumpkineater Imperial Pumpkin Ale, and Pothole Filler Imperial Stout, all of which top out above 7.5% ABV and offer big, robust flavour profiles.

That said, don't skip out on their regular brews in favour of trying the monster imperials—Mitchell's original bitter recipe, Baldwin & Cooper Best Bitter, is worth the trip to Squamish alone. For that matter, I do recommend going to the brewpub in person. Stay overnight, enjoy a meal in the restaurant and a nightcap at the pub listening to a local band. Wake up to the incredible views of the Chief, maybe even go for a climb or a hike, and then buy some bottles to bring home with you. Howe Sound is one of B.C.'s top craft beer getaways.

Facts & Figures

OPENED ▸ *1996* ✪ **STYLES PRODUCED ▸** *7 + seasonals* ✪
WHERE TO BUY ▸ *Liquor stores throughout B.C. and at the brewery* ✪
ON TAP ▸ *Throughout B.C.* ✪ **GROWLERS ▸** *No*

www.whistlerbeer.com
604-962-8889
1045 Millar Creek Road
Whistler
E-MAIL tours@whistlerbeer.com

Whistler Brewing

|||||||||||||||||||||||||||||||||||||||||||||

WHEN I FIRST arrived in B.C. in 1991, Whistler Brewing's Black Tusk Ale quickly became one of my favourite beers. Unfortunately, after a few short years, it seemed to disappear off the market. Over the two decades since then, Black Tusk and other Whistler beers have come and gone as the company has moved through several ownership changes, resulting in inconsistent brews and a lack of brand confidence among beer drinkers. Even today, calling Whistler Brewing a "craft brewery" is debatable, and depends on your individual interpretation of that designation. (See "You're Soaking in It" on page 195 for more on that dilemma.)

In 1999, the brewery merged with Bowen Island Brewing and the new company moved to Delta. By 2001, the Whistler brand was being produced by Bear Brewing in Kamloops. Alberta's Big Rock Brewing bought Bear and the other brands in 2003 as part of an attempt to gain a foothold in the B.C. beer market, but by 2005, Big Rock was disillusioned with that plan and sold the brands to the NorthAm Group, based in Vancouver, which revitalized the Whistler brand with an eye to the coming Winter Olympics in 2010. They still brewed the beer in Kamloops, but

Tap List

BLACK TUSK ALE
5% ABV
This Dark Mild has stood the test of time.

WHISKEY JACK ALE
5% ABV
A basic, inoffensive amber ale.

PARADISE VALLEY GRAPEFRUIT ALE (seasonal)
5% ABV
A twist on the idea of adding a slice of something citrusy to a wheat beer, this is a blonde ale with added grapefruit rind. Interesting.

VALLEY TRAIL CHESTNUT ALE (seasonal)
5% ABV
Personally I find this beer overly sweet and virtually undrinkable, but some friends swear it is delicious—this one's for you, Glen!

claimed to use Whistler glacier water, shipped all the way by tanker truck. I've heard from more than a few industry insiders that they really did ship water there from Whistler—but I still have trouble believing it myself.

Beer drinkers in Whistler were not impressed with the pretence of a beer with their hometown's name on it that was actually brewed three hundred kilometres away, so in 2009, just in time for the Olympics, the brewery opened a small brewhouse in the Function Junction industrial neighbourhood, about fifteen minutes south of Whistler Village and its world-famous ski hills. Most Whistler beer is still brewed in Kamloops, but at least some of it is now produced in the town itself. The Function Junction location has a taphouse with a basic food menu and a fun but surprisingly expensive tour that is geared towards people who know little or nothing about brewing. If you're a beer geek who already knows the difference between a lauter tun and a brite tank, forgo forking over $13.95 for the tour and buy a six-pack of Black Tusk Ale instead.

The current version of Black Tusk Ale is pretty good; Whistler claims it is the original recipe, but twenty years later, I have no way of knowing whether this is true or even possible. I doubt it, but regardless, it's their best beer.

....
Facts & Figures

OPENED ▸ *1989 (& 1999 & 2001 & 2006 & 2009 …)* ✪ **STYLES PRODUCED ▸** *5 + seasonals* ✪ **WHERE TO BUY ▸** *Liquor stores throughout B.C. and at the brewery* ✪ **ON TAP ▸** *Throughout B.C.* ✪ **GROWLERS ▸** *Yes*

JOHN MITCHELL

The Grandfather of Craft Beer
in British Columbia

....

JOHN MITCHELL is a crotchety curmudgeon. There is simply no better way to describe him, except perhaps in his own words, "A bloody, brainless fool," as he referred to himself several times during our conversation at Howe Sound Brewing in August 2012, on the first day of my Craft Beer Odyssey.

At eighty-two years of age, having accomplished what he has, much of it through sheer dogged determination, it's not surprising he is cantankerous in his twilight years. But he also has a great affection for Howe Sound, his "local," which he visits every Friday, as well as its co-owner and CEO, Leslie Fenn. She treats him like visiting royalty every time and has seemingly infinite patience with him, even when he is critiquing the beer and *tsking* over its serving temperatures after testing it with the thermometer he carries in his shirt pocket.

Mitchell's beer of choice, a Baldwin & Cooper ESB, his original recipe when he set up the brewery there back in 1996, is delicious: a pitch-perfect bitter, one of the best examples of the style you'll find in B.C. And he still likes it, too—once it has warmed up to "proper cellar temperature," that is.

Born in England, Mitchell trained as a chef at the Mayfair Hotel in post-war London. He also spent three months working in the cellar there, delivering Worthington's White Shield beer to the various pubs, restaurants and dining rooms throughout the hotel. This was bottle-conditioned beer that had to rest in the cellar for forty-eight hours after delivery.

"You had to handle them like bloody bombs," Mitchell says. That was when he first began to understand the idea of real beer as being alive. "For my pleasure, Stan the cellar man, bless his heart, would give me a bottle every day. That, to me, was the Rolls Royce of beer. I've never forgotten it."

Bottle-conditioned beer in England, though once the standard, has pretty much gone the way of the dodo, but thankfully, Mitchell's early experience with it contributed to the renaissance in "real beer" production he helped ignite in Canada some thirty years later.

When he immigrated to Canada in 1954, Mitchell says, "I thought I'd stepped back into Prohibition." The beer scene was horrible then, he says, with essentially no choice between the three dominant brewers, Carling, Labatt and Molson.

In 1978, Mitchell had been the bar manager at the Sylvia Hotel in Vancouver's West End for fifteen years when he and a neighbour had the opportunity to take over the Troller Pub in Horseshoe Bay, where he lived. Back then, he says, the liquor board assigned pubs one of the three big breweries to ensure balance between them, and the Troller was arbitrarily connected with Carling.

When brewery workers went on strike in 1979, "There was no beer in the middle of the summer," for several weeks. The Troller was forced to serve cider until the liquor board finally brought in Olympia Beer from the U.S. "I was so incensed," he says.

Remembering the beer culture he grew up in back in Britain, Mitchell "went on a pilgrimage" to the only four remaining traditional brewpubs in England in 1980. Back in B.C., he persuaded his business partners that they should build their own brewery. They grudgingly agreed to let him pursue it, but first he had to persuade Allan Gould, the manager of the Liquor Distribution Board.

As Mitchell puts it, he "ranted and raved" at Gould for forty-five minutes, expecting to be turfed out with a simple no afterwards, but instead, he says Gould's response was, "Well, John, I've been trying to think of reasons to turn you down and

I haven't thought of one. Now you have to put a proposal in to the minister."

Mitchell submitted his application in May 1981. As fortune would have it, the minister, Peter Hyndman, was already frustrated with apparent collusion between the three big national breweries, and he likely saw Mitchell's request as a positive PR opportunity. When one of the breweries raised its prices slightly that summer and the other two dutifully followed suit, Hyndman had had enough. According to Mitchell, the minister pulled out his proposal in front of reporters and said he was going to allow it. Mitchell first heard about it from a CBC reporter who called him up to ask about the new brewery, and then he received a call from Gould who told him he had to build his brewery now.

Knowing nothing about brewing, Mitchell turned to Frank Appleton, another British ex-pat who had written an article in *Harrowsmith* about brewing. Appleton had worked at Carling-O'Keefe's for several years before quitting over the inferior quality of the beers. Mitchell managed to persuade Appleton to join him in Horseshoe Bay and the two put together the rudimentary brewery using dairy equipment for about $35,000. They had to put the brewery in a separate building from the pub—federal law required it to be at least a roadway away.

His partners, aghast at the price tag, asked him how much beer they'd have to sell to break even. He thought one keg a day would cover it, but they were only selling two kegs of Carling per day at best.

The beer they brewed—arguably the first modern-day craft beer brewed in Canada—was Bay Ale, a British Mild modelled after Fuller's London Pride. Mitchell says he delivered eight kegs to the pub on the first day. They sold seven. Now his partners insisted he had to brew a lot more, but the tiny brewery could only manage to produce thirty kegs per week, which meant the pub could only sell five per day, since it was open six days a week.

They rarely managed to keep up with demand. On one memorable evening, a soccer team from Richmond decided to hire a bus "to go to Horseshoe Bay for a decent pint." They showed up at 7:00 PM, but that day's five kegs were gone already so the team was out of luck.

Mitchell says the brewery paid back its $35,000 cost in just twelve weeks and was making the pub $500 per day in clear profit. He brewed all the beer for a while, but after a series of disagreements with his partners, he left at the end of 1982 to join Paul Hadfield and another business partner in setting up a new brewpub on the waterfront in Victoria. That was Spinnakers, which opened in 1984 and is still thriving today while Horseshoe Bay Brewing only lasted for a few years.

Having learned his lesson with the cobbled-together brewing equipment he'd made do with at Horseshoe Bay, Mitchell bought a proper system from England for Spinnakers. He brewed four beers to start: Spinnakers Ale, a light ale meant for mainstream drinkers; Mitchell's ESB, which is still being served there today; Mt. Tolmie Dark Ale; and Empress Stout. The brewpub was a big hit and continues to be to this day. In the 1988 edition of his *New World Guide to Beer*, famed British beer critic Michael Jackson describes Mitchell's ESB as "beautifully balanced," the Mt. Tolmie Dark as "a classic strong mild, of which Britain should be envious," and the Empress Stout as "a model of the style."

Unfortunately, Mitchell had another falling-out with this set of business partners and left Spinnakers after two and a half years. It must be said that he was probably not the easiest person to get along with, at least in his approach to business, considering the disputes he had with his partners at both Horseshoe Bay and Spinnakers—he certainly feels like he was taken advantage of in both situations. At least he ended his association with the microbrewing scene on a positive note when he helped set up Howe Sound Brewing in Squamish. Yes, he is quick to point out any flaw or inconsistency there, too, but he still shows up every Friday without fail and is welcomed with open arms.

B.C.'s craft beer revolution owes its start to the dogged determination of "this idiot Mitchell," to use another of his colourful self-descriptions. Arguably, taking on the brewing triumvirate of Carling, Labatt and Molson and the bureaucratic indifference of various levels of government in the early 1980s required someone who was stubborn almost to the point of being pig-headed, which is precisely what he was.

"My loud mouth got me some attention and it worked," he says now, looking back to thirty years ago when everything started at Horseshoe Bay. And of B.C.'s craft beer revolution and the part he played in it? "I'm very proud of what has happened. I couldn't be more pleased."

Thank you, John.

BEST BEERS

Sea-to-Sky

• •

BrewHouse High Mountain Brewing 5 Rings IPA
Voted best IPA at the 2012 B.C. Beer Awards: it's worth the trip
to Whistler alone.

Bridge Brewing North Shore Pale
A delicious pale ale with a solid Northwest hop profile.

Howe Sound Brewing King Heffy Imperial Hefeweizen
Warning: after one taste, you will not stop until this entire
one-litre bottle is empty. And then you might want to open
another...

Howe Sound Brewing Pumpkineater Imperial Pumpkin Ale
The best pumpkin beer in B.C. with a deep malty flavour tinged
with roasted pumpkin: not cloyingly sweet like too many other
pumpkin beers.

Howe Sound Brewing Total Eclipse of the Hop
This imperial IPA packs a wallop of flavour: a deep, rich malty
backbone supports a decadent array of hops

2

★ VICTORIA ★

AT THE BREWERY	DRAFT	FOOD	GROWLERS	BOTTLE SALES	TOURS	BEDS
Canoe Brewpub	★	★	★	★	★	
Driftwood Brewing			★			
Hoyne Brewing			★	★	★	
Lighthouse Brewing			★	★	★	
Moon Under Water	★	★	★	★	★	
Phillips Brewing			★	★	★	
Spinnakers Gastro Brewpub	★	★	★	★		★
Swans Brewpub	★	★		★		★
Vancouver Island Brewing			★	★	★	

CAPITAL CRAFT

....

BREWING IN B.C. dates back to 1858, the same year British Columbia became a province, when William Steinberger opened Victoria Brewing on the shores of Swan Lake, just north of Victoria. The German immigrant had come to North America in search of gold, but he saw a business opportunity when he realized the burgeoning new capital of B.C. had no breweries of its own.

A similar opportunity was seized by Paul Hadfield, John Mitchell and their business partners back in 1984 when they opened Canada's first modern-day brewpub on the shore of Victoria's picturesque Inner Harbour, kicking open the door to the craft beer revolution in Canada that had been initiated by Mitchell and Frank Appleton in Horseshoe Bay two years earlier. While Hadfield initially saw Spinnakers mainly as an architectural project, he later took over as publican there and has been in charge of the seminal B.C. brewery ever since.

But the craft beer scene in Victoria goes way beyond Spinnakers. Three other excellent brewpubs have followed Spinnakers' lead over the years, all within an easy mile-long walking loop around the Upper Harbour above the fabled Blue Bridge. Add five top-notch craft breweries and another brew-pub in the works at the Four Mile Pub in nearby View Royal, and the result is the best single beer destination in the province—although Vancouver is catching up quickly and may take over that distinction in 2013 with all the new breweries about to open there.

Victoria's pubs and restaurants are definitely devoted to their breweries; you'll find local beers on tap almost anywhere you go, while B.C.'s other craft breweries are not nearly as well represented. That is slowly starting to change with the emergence of a taphouse culture, driven by local consumers' desire for more variety.

There are some great stories to go along with the excellent beer being crafted: the legendary Matt Phillips who started his brewery by maxing out every credit card he could get when the banks all turned down his loan applications; the incredible success story of Driftwood Brewery, which has gone from fledgling newbie to darling of many of the province's craft beer geeks in four short years; and the long road Sean Hoyne took from brewing at Swans and the Canoe for more than twenty years before finally starting his own brewery in 2011.

You can sleep above the brewpub at Swans or next door from the pub at Spinnakers; canoe, kayak or take the Victoria Harbour Ferry between the four brewpubs; check out the breweries with a tour and tasting at Phillips or Vancouver Island Brewing; and fill your growler at nearly every brewery and brewpub in town. Victoria is more than just the provincial capital—it's B.C.'s Craft Beer Capital, too.

www.canoebrewpub.com
250-361-1940
450 Swift Street, Victoria
E-MAIL info@canoebrewpub.com

Canoe Brewpub, Marina and Restaurant

||||||||||||||||||||||||||||||||||||||||||

CANOE MIGHT JUST be the best place to drink a beer in British Columbia—architecturally speaking, at least. The brewpub is situated in a gorgeous heritage edifice, the brick-clad City Lights Building (built in 1894), which originally housed coal-fired generators that powered the city's streetlights. Following a $6-million restoration, it boasts dramatic vaulted ceilings and exposed beams, with the pub and restaurant split into separate areas so that each room feels intimate and self-contained despite the size of the building. The Canoe also has the city's best west-facing patio, ideal for soaking in the rays come summertime, right down on the edge of the Upper Harbour with a great view of the old Blue Bridge (which may or may not be still there by the time you read this as there is an ongoing political fight over restoring or replacing it).

Officially, the name of the place is the Canoe Brewpub, Marina and Restaurant, and yes, you can arrive by sailboat, kayak or canoe at the short-term dinghy dock. The brewpub is also a stop on the Victoria Harbour Ferry route so you can catch a lift up to the Moon Under Water brewpub one stop north at Point Ellice Historic House

Tap List

BEAVER BROWN ALE
5.4% ABV | 18 IBU
Full-bodied and creamy but not heavy. Very drinkable and satisfying.

RIVER ROCK BITTER
5.2% ABV | 25 IBU
An excellent bitter with a copper colour and a balanced malt-hop bitterness.

GOLDEN LION BELGIAN ALE (seasonal)
5.6% ABV | 15 IBU
An exceptional Belgian golden ale with spicy, fruity flavours and a rich malt character.

SOUTHERN CROSS IPA (seasonal)
5.5% ABV | 75 IBU
This South Pacific IPA bursts with hops from Australia and New Zealand that offer tropical fruit-tinged bitterness.

or head south into the Inner Harbour and get dropped off at Spinnakers.

Sean Hoyne, the original brewer at Swans, became the brewmaster at Canoe when it opened and stayed there for fourteen years before he finally launched his own brewery in 2011. Replacing Sean is Daniel Murphy who brings an Australian accent and flavour to the place. Murphy apprenticed under Hoyne for several years before working at a brewery in Tasmania where he says an exciting nascent craft beer scene is just starting to take off. He has already put his own unique spin on the beer lineup, introducing an IPA made with hops from Australia and New Zealand, along with other special seasonals including an excellent Belgian golden ale.

The Canoe Brewpub has a top-notch kitchen to go along with its strong assortment of beers, making it a destination for foodies as well as beer lovers. There is a strong focus on local ingredients, and they also host occasional Brewmaster Dinners with the food courses paired with specific beers.

Facts & Figures

OPENED ▸ *1996* ✪ STYLES PRODUCED ▸ *4 + seasonals* ✪ WHERE TO BUY ▸ *In bottles at the brewpub* ✪ ON TAP ▸ *The brewpub* ✪ GROWLERS ▸ *Yes*

FROM SWAN LAKE
TO SPRING RIDGE

The Early Days
of Brewing in Victoria

••••••••••••••••••••••••

WILLIAM STEINBERGER came to North America from Köln, Germany, seeking a lucky strike in the California gold rush. As he followed the crowds of prospectors north to B.C.'s Cariboo gold fields, he realized there was another, better way to make some money—brewing beer for the thirsty crowds in Victoria, a boomtown which had seen its population jump from three hundred to five thousand as it became the supply hub for prospectors heading north. So, in 1858, he purchased some excess grain from a local farm that had lost its Russian market because of the Crimean War, and established Western Canada's first brewery on the shores of Swan Lake, just north of Victoria.

The next year, he built a larger operation in downtown Victoria (probably because the murky waters of Swan Lake would not have been ideal for brewing) and within a few years his Victoria Brewing Company was joined by five others. It must have helped when the British Royal Navy set up its base in Esquimalt in 1865—then, as now, sailors proved a good source of thirsty customers. Steinberger himself did not stick around very long, but other brewers who followed him did and some became quite prominent citizens as Victoria grew from rugged fort to provincial capital.

The brewers' demand for ingredients led to a hop-growing industry on the Saanich Peninsula that became so large, the farms were even exporting their hops off-island for a time. Unfortunately, they were decimated by a hop louse infestation in the 1890s and the industry died out there. Barley was not a very successful crop because of the damp climate so it had to be imported.

Several breweries in Victoria set up shop on Spring Ridge—present-day Fernwood—to make use of the clean, flowing spring water there. The earliest recorded one was the Lion Brewery, which opened in 1862, but others also built breweries in the area, or piped the water to their operations downtown.

After the turn of the century, the most prominent breweries in the city were the Victoria-Phoenix (after the 1893 merging of Steinberger's original enterprise, which had changed hands several times already, with Phoenix Brewery) and Silver Spring Brewery, which was founded in 1902 in Vic West. Those two companies dominated the market until 1928 when they were amalgamated under the Coast Breweries banner and began brewing Lucky Lager to compete with Molson and Labatt.

Labatt bought Lucky Lager Breweries in 1958. They demolished the Silver Spring brewery in 1962, but continued to brew Lucky at the original Victoria-Phoenix plant downtown on Government Street until 1981. Even though the company had initiated a major heritage renovation in the '70s, Labatt levelled the historic building in 1982, ending local production of Lucky Lager, or any beer, in Victoria.

The city was only "dry" for two years, though, until 1984 when both Spinnakers and Vancouver Island Brewery (then Coast Pacific Brewing) opened.

www.driftwoodbeer.com
250-381-2739
102-450 Hillside Avenue
Victoria
E-MAIL orders@driftwoodbeer.com
TWITTER @driftwoodbeer

Driftwood Brewery

Tap List

FARMHAND ALE

5.5% ABV

A full-bodied saison with
a spicy Belgian yeast character and a peppery zing
you'll feel in your sinuses.
Unique and delicious.

FAT TUG IPA

7% ABV | 80 IBU

Arguably the best beer in
B.C. A big hop profile featuring citrus and pine from
a "shwack o' hops," as the
label reads.

SARTORI HARVEST

IPA (seasonal)

7% ABV | 75 IBU

Brewed with "wet hops"
immediately after the
harvest, this IPA features
fresh, grassy, citrusy hop
flavours. Exceptional and
very popular.

SINGULARITY (seasonal)

11.8% ABV

This bourbon barrel–aged
Russian imperial stout
features complex flavours
including plums, berries,
chocolate, caramel and
port. Simply incredible.

||||||||||||||||||||||||||||||||||||||||||||||

KEVIN HEARSUM AND JASON MEYER met while
working together as assistant brewers at
Lighthouse Brewing, where they spent a
lot of time fantasizing about what they'd
do if they had their own brewery. That
dream became a reality when they opened
Driftwood in late 2008. Even in their wildest fantasies, however, I doubt they ever
expected to achieve the level of success they
have in such a short time. In their first four
years they established the brewery as one of
B.C.'s best—*the* best according to many of the
province's hard-core beer geeks.

The brewing duo had a solid plan to set
Driftwood apart. "We wanted to stake out
our space as a brewer of Belgian beers in
the Northwest," Meyer told me shortly after
they opened. Of their first three beers, two
were Belgians: a wit called White Bark Ale
and Farmhand Ale, a saison brewed with 10
per cent sour mash and cracked pepper. The
third was a Northwest pale ale, simply called
Driftwood Ale. That trio still represents the
core of Driftwood's lineup, but since then the
brewery has added Crooked Coast Amber
Ale and several interesting seasonals. Oh
yeah, I almost forgot, they also brew a little
IPA you've probably never heard of called
Fat Tug.

It was the addition of Fat Tug IPA in late 2010 that cata-pulted Driftwood to the upper echelons of B.C.'s beer scene. Before they launched it, Meyer told me, "There are a lot of good IPAs out there. We know that the bar has been set high, so we intend to try and set it just a little bit higher." Audacious words, perhaps, but that's exactly what they did. Fat Tug has quickly grown into their flagship beer, accounting for 40 per cent of their sales. It is so wildly popular in the Vancouver area that the brewery had to open its own warehouse there and hire sales staff who just focus on the Lower Mainland.

Other Driftwood beers are extremely popular as well: their annual wet-hopped seasonal, Sartori Harvest IPA, is the most highly anticipated seasonal release in B.C. (see "Hopping Fresh" on page 38); and Singularity, a potent, barrel-aged imperial stout they release each January, is coveted and hoarded by craft beer cellarists. The brewery has also initiated a sour beer program called "Bird of Prey," which has featured a Flanders red ale and a blended sour brown ale called Mad Bruin.

Talk about a dream come true—for the Driftwood team as well as B.C.'s beer lovers.

Facts & Figures

OPENED ▸ *2008* ✪ **STYLES PRODUCED** ▸ *5 + seasonals* ✪ **WHERE TO BUY** ▸ *Liquor stores throughout B.C.* ✪ **ON TAP** ▸ *Throughout B.C.* ✪ **GROWLERS** ▸ *Yes*

HOPPING FRESH

The most popular
seasonal beer style in B.C.

....

THERE ARE SEVERAL different seasonal beers brewed in B.C., including berry beers made with fresh, local raspberries each summer and pumpkin beers fermented with sugar pumpkins each fall. But the single seasonal style that garners the most excitement in the craft beer community each year is one that is tied into the annual hop harvest that occurs at summer's end.

Fresh-hopped or wet-hopped beers, as they are sometimes called, use hops that have just been harvested and are still dripping with the succulent oils that contribute so much aroma, flavour and bitterness to beer. Normally, hops are dried so that they can be shipped and stored for several months without spoiling. Instead, fresh-hopped beers must be brewed as quickly as possible after the hops have been picked.

The most exciting and sought-after fresh-hopped beer in B.C. each fall is Driftwood Brewery's Sartori Harvest IPA, which the brewery first produced in 2009 and has released annually ever since. Although Driftwood is on Vancouver Island, the brewers travel to the mainland to load their truck with fresh hops from the Sartori Cedar Ranch in Chilliwack, then drive back to the brewery and brew the batch first thing the next morning.

Driftwood adds fresh hops at multiple points during the brewing process, with the result being a unique beer that showcases the hops' freshest qualities above and beyond anything else. In other words: a hophead's wildest fantasy. But it is an ephemeral style, not ideal for cellaring, because the volatile hop oils and flavour compounds break down quickly. This is a beer to drink soon after you get it. After more than a few months, it won't taste nearly as good.

Driftwood Brewery may not have been the first B.C. brewery to release a wet-hopped beer, but Sartori Harvest IPA has quickly become the brand that is synonymous with the style in B.C., and rightfully so. While it is difficult to compare wet-hopped beers because they have a limited run and they don't last very long, Driftwood's annual release has been excellent each year.

Usually, Sartori features a big nose of sweet citrus and grassy aromas that are just as prominent in the flavour of the beer, too. Underneath all those amazing, mouth-watering, fresh aromas, it's a solid IPA comparable to their incomparable Fat Tug IPA, but with a fresh zing.

Other B.C. breweries produce fresh-hopped beers, too. Salt Spring Island Ales actually has its own hops field on a farm just over a kilometre from their brewery. They hold a harvest festival there and add the fresh hops to a different style in their lineup each year. Spinnakers uses hops grown on its own farm in Sooke in a variety of fresh-hopped beers each fall.

Here are a few other B.C. breweries that release fresh-hopped beers each fall (available mid-September to mid-October):

Granville Island Brewing (Vancouver)
Fresh Hop ESB

Hoyne Brewing (Victoria)
Wolf Vine Wet-Hopped Pale Ale

Phillips Brewing (Victoria)
Green Reaper IPA

Townsite Brewing (Powell River)
Time Warp Wet-Hopped Pale Ale

www.hoynebrewing.com
250-590-5758
101-2740 Bridge Street
Victoria
E-MAIL info@hoynebrewing.ca
TWITTER @hoynebeer

Hoyne Brewing

||||||||||||||||||||||||||||||||||||||||||||

SEAN HOYNE has been a professional brewer in Victoria longer than anyone else—surprising since he never planned on brewing beer for a living. He was studying graduate-level literature at the University of Victoria and brewing beer at home on the side back in 1989 when he saw an ad seeking a brewer at the brand-new Swans Brewpub. He applied on a whim and brought a six-pack of his homebrew to the interview with Frank Appleton, who designed and built the brewery.

Appleton, who, together with John Mitchell, was one of the founding fathers of B.C.'s modern craft brewing movement (see "John Mitchell" on page 22), had helped with the construction of the brewpub but was ready to hand over the reins to a worthy apprentice. Hoyne says that the interview with Appleton amounted to drinking his homebrews and chatting about them; by the time the bottles were empty, he'd been offered the job.

Hoyne quickly realized he had found his true calling. He spent several years at Swans before moving on to open the Canoe brewpub just down the street, where he worked for the next fourteen years. He wanted to open his own brewery ever since he got into

Tap List

HOYNER PILSNER
5.5% ABV
An authentic Bohemian Pilsner, this is bursting with flavour well beyond its light appearance.

DARK MATTER
5.3% ABV
Not a porter. Not a stout. This mysterious brew is surprisingly quaffable for such a dark beer.

DEVIL'S DREAM IPA
6% ABV
A well-balanced West Coast IPA with a solid malt foundation that really shows off the pine/citrus hops.

GRATITUDE (seasonal)
9% ABV
Beautifully packaged in seasonal paper, this full-bodied winter warmer is ideal for carolling parties and late-night gift-wrapping sessions.

the business, and the recent craft beer boom in B.C. helped solidify his decision to finally make the leap.

It took him only eight months to get his brewery up and running in a building right next to Driftwood Brewery in the semi-industrial Rock Bay area of Victoria, which is also home to the Moon Under Water brewpub. Although the location isn't exactly trendy, the brewery sells a lot of beer in growlers—it's always busy at the filling station whenever I swing by to get a refill.

Hoyne is dedicated to each beer style he brews, envisioning his ideal consumer as someone who loves that specific style first and foremost. So, for instance, his Pilsner is a true Bohemian Pilsner, bursting with flavour despite its light appearance, and wouldn't be out of place in a pub in the Czech Republic. His IPA, though not as over-the-top hoppy as some other West Coast versions, still boasts a citrus-pine nose and a flavour with a great malt-hop balance.

The bottle labels feature poetic discursions, definitely showing off Hoyne's literary origins. Apparently, he still likes to catch up on the latest critical perspectives on James Joyce's *Ulysses*, but now, at least, it's with a glass of his own Dark Matter or Down Easy Pale Ale in hand.

Facts & Figures

OPENED ▸ *2011* ✪ **STYLES PRODUCED ▸** *5 + seasonals* ✪ **WHERE TO BUY ▸** *At the brewery, and in Vancouver Island and Lower Mainland liquor stores* ✪ **ON TAP ▸** *Vancouver Island and Vancouver* ✪ **GROWLERS ▸** *Yes*

www.lighthousebrewing.com
250-383-6500
836 Devonshire Road, Victoria
E-MAIL info@lighthousebrewing.com
TWITTER @lighthousebeer

Lighthouse Brewing

||||||||||||||||||||||||||||||||||||||||||||||

I WAS LIVING in Victoria in 1998 when Race Rocks Amber Ale, Lighthouse's flagship beer, first appeared, and it immediately became my favourite local beer. It was dark but not heavy, very drinkable with a malt character balanced between caramel and roasted barley. I moved away from Victoria a few years later and discovered other new beers, but when my girlfriend and I decided to get married in Victoria where we'd met, it was an easy decision to serve Race Rocks at the reception.

Lighthouse was founded by Paul Hoyne, brother to another local brewer, Sean Hoyne. It has grown significantly over the years, and underwent a major expansion in 2012. Up until a few years ago, though, Lighthouse was dismissed by many craft beer drinkers. Their core lineup was safe and innocuous, and none of their beers reflected the new trends in craft beer—West Coast IPAS, Belgian styles and the like. Television ads that featured guys ogling bikini babes didn't help much either.

That all changed with the launch of their Big Flavour series in 2010, which showcased beer geek styles in 650 mL bombers—including Shipwrecked Triple IPA, Navigator

Tap List

**RACE ROCKS
AMBER ALE**
5% ABV
This dark amber ale is very quaffable with a lighter body than its colour implies.

TASMAN ALE
5% ABV
A copper-coloured ale tinged with tropical flavours from exotic Tasmanian hops. One of the best labels around, too.

SWITCHBACK IPA
6.5% ABV | 85 IBU
One of the top three West Coast IPAs in B.C. with a heady blend of citrusy, aromatic Citra, Zythos and Falconer's Flight hops.

**SIREN RED
ALE** (seasonal)
8% ABV | 70 IBU
A big, bold, boozy, malty, yeasty and hoppy beer that doesn't really fit any stylistic description I can think of other than: delicious.

Doppelbock, Deckhand Belgian Saison, Overboard Imperial Pilsner and Uncharted Belgian IPA—all with original labels painted by local artists. And indeed, the beer geeks took notice. Each new release was met with much pleasure and discussion.

Then, in early 2012, Lighthouse took it up another notch with the release of Belgian Black in a striking all-black bottle featuring a white skeletal pirate. As beautiful as the image was, what was in the bottle caught the most attention. Though it came out early in January, some Vancouver beer bloggers declared it the year's best brew. It was darn good. The unique Ardennes yeast that brewer Dean McLeod used pulled plum and cherry flavours out of the dark malts and merged them with that spicy character unique to Belgian yeasts. Truly exceptional. A few months later, Lighthouse followed it up with Belgian White, an imperial wit beer that used the same yeast along with some Northwest hops (Galaxy and Citra) to impart a citrusy zing. And late in the year, they continued the colour theme with Siren Imperial Red Ale, which might just have been the best of the bunch.

While this big-bottle series certainly helped restore Lighthouse's reputation, I think their release of Switchback IPA as a core brand in six-packs secured them a spot in the upper echelon of B.C. brewers. It's a true West Coast IPA with a great body, a citrus-pine aroma and an assertive bitterness. They could have released it as a special edition bomber, but the fact that it is available in government liquor stores and on tap year-round makes me very happy indeed.

Facts & Figures

OPENED › *1998* ✪ **STYLES PRODUCED ›** *8 + seasonals* ✪ **WHERE TO BUY ›** *Liquor stores throughout B.C.* ✪ **ON TAP ›** *Victoria-area restaurants and select spots in Vancouver* ✪ **GROWLERS ›** *Yes*

www.moonunderwater.ca
250-380-0706
350B Bay Street, Victoria
E-MAIL moonunderwater@shaw.ca
TWITTER @TheMoonBrewpub

The Moon Under Water

IIIIIIIIIIIIIIIIIIIIIIIIIIIIIIIIIIIIIIIIIIIIIII

If you are asked why you favour a particular public-house, it would seem natural to put the beer first, but the thing that most appeals to me about the Moon Under Water is what people call its 'atmosphere.' GEORGE ORWELL, "The Moon Under Water," *Evening Standard*, February 9, 1946

Tap List

POTTS PILS

5.2% ABV | 38 IBU

An authentic, unfiltered North German Pilsner: light, dry and crisp. *Sehr gut!*

CREEPY UNCLE DUNKEL

5.4% ABV

Dunkels are not very well known here, but this slightly sweet dark lager is exactly what you'd find on tap in Germany.

TRANQUILITY IPA

6.5% ABV | 70 IBU

Updated from the brewpub's original British version, Potts calls this a "Canadian IPA."

VICTORIOUS WEIZENBOCK

8.2% ABV

Wow, this is a bold brew: spicy yeast flavours underneath a marvelously complex malty body.

FOUNDED BY Don and Bonnie Bradley (who founded Bowen Island Brewing in the 1990s) along with their nephew Ron, Victoria's newest brewpub is named after Orwell's fictional ideal of what a pub should be. The Bradleys' aim, according to the website, was to create "a little oasis in the middle of the Rock Bay industrial area that has a comfortable and inviting atmosphere. A place for real social networking and to enjoy conversation beside the fireplace." They started off brewing low-gravity British-style session ales, including a full-bodied bitter with only 3.8 per cent ABV, just as one might expect to find in a British pub.

Although I enjoyed meeting the Bradleys and tasting their beer on my first visit to the pub, I found its atmosphere unappealing. Its location in a non-descript building in Victoria's industrial area was a big part of the problem. Inside, the décor and furnishings were not in line with the kind of heritage character that a traditional British pub demands. The beer was fine, especially when they added a fairly hoppy IPA into the mix. But I just never had the urge to go there like I did with Swans, Spinnakers or the Canoe.

Just after the 2012 Great Canadian Beer Festival, the pub suddenly changed ownership. The new owners, a young couple named Clay Potter and Chelsea Walker, began tweaking the style of the place to "turn it into craft beer central." Born and raised in Victoria, Potter worked at Lighthouse and Driftwood before going to Scotland to study brewing and distilling at Heriot-Watt University (a route that several young B.C. brewers have taken in recent years).

Potter fell in love with German beers during an internship at a big Bitburger brewery and has shifted the beer lineup to include some authentic Pilsners and wheat beers alongside the core IPA. He also hopes to add some bottle-conditioned imperial styles to the mix. He was about to brew an imperial pumpkin ale when I visited and was also fermenting a crop of pears from a friend's orchard that he planned to add to some wheat beer left over from the previous owners.

Potter and Walker decided to keep the pub's name the same so as not to alienate existing customers, but they have distinctly rebranded it as "The Moon." They also want to set up a brewing research and education centre there, bringing in guest speakers and encouraging collaborations with other brewers. They already had three guest taps on and plan on adding three more so there will eventually be six guest beers along with the six brewed there.

....

Facts & Figures

OPENED ▸ *2011* ✪ **STYLES PRODUCED** ▸ *4 + seasonals* ✪
WHERE TO BUY ▸ *The brewpub and private liquor stores in Victoria and Vancouver* ✪ **ON TAP** ▸ *The brewpub* ✪
GROWLERS ▸ *Yes*

GREAT CANADIAN
BEER FESTIVAL

....

Held every September on the Friday and Saturday after Labour Day

THE BIGGEST annual event on the B.C. craft beer calendar and one of the biggest in Canada along with Montreal's Mondiale du Bière, the Great Canadian Beer Festival celebrated its twentieth anniversary in 2012 and just keeps getting better and better—despite numerous obstacles thrown in its path by government bureaucrats over the years.

From its humble origins in the Victoria Convention Centre in 1993 to its mammoth current proportions on the soccer pitch at Royal Athletic Park, this festival has certainly come a long way over the years. These days, more than eight thousand people attend over two days, sampling beers from fifty-five breweries from throughout Canada and the U.S. The entry ticket includes a sample glass (unfortunately plastic because of liquor authorities concerned about breakage and injuries) and a program featuring profiles of all the beers on hand. Tokens for beer samples are sold inside the event.

Tickets go on sale in July and sell out very quickly. Plan a long weekend in Victoria around the GCBF and visit some of the excellent brewpubs and breweries B.C.'s Craft Capital has to offer.

www.gcbf.com

GROWLIN'
FOR BEER

....

MY WIFE and I travelled to New York City on our "babymoon" (the final trip before the arrival of a baby) back in the summer of 2008. Walking through Chinatown and Little Italy one afternoon we stumbled across a nondescript place with a plain green awning that read "New Beer Distributors. All brands beer and soda. Since 1968. Open to the public." Inside, we found a big warehouse jammed with shelves all covered in bottles and cans of beer from around the world. My pregnant and therefore teetotalling wife allowed me to stay in this paradise for fifteen minutes; I just wandered through aisle after aisle looking at so many beers I'd never even heard of before.

On the way out I saw something else I'd never seen before: a row of taps where you could fill a jug with whatever beer they had on tap that week. This was my first encounter with a growler, although I didn't even know the name of it then.

A growler is a big glass bottle with a handle on the neck that resembles a moonshine jug. The regular size is 1.89 litres, which is half a gallon. That works out to a little less than a typical six-pack or about four 16-ounce U.S. pints, which is the typical size of a "sleeve" of beer in B.C. (unless the pub is serving authentic British pints, which are 20 ounces). The concept behind growlers is that you buy the jug itself (usually $5–$7) and then pay for a fill of whatever beer you like ($10–$12 per fill). Since it is usually filled simply from a draft tap and then hand-sealed with a plastic cap, it will only last about a week in the fridge at home, and a day or two once you've cracked the seal. Then, once you've emptied it, rinse it out and bring it back to the brewery where you bought it—or another brewery that fills growlers—for a refill. This time, you'll only pay for the fill, not for the growler itself. (It's not a deposit system; breweries will not accept the bottle for a refund.)

The name "growler" has an interesting origin. According to the *Oxford Companion to Beer*, back in the late 1800s and early 1900s, most beer was consumed on draft in American cities. If people wanted to bring beer home, the container most often used was a galvanized steel pail with a lid on it to prevent spillage. That lid would rumble or "growl" as carbonation escaped, and the name growler was born. There was even an expression for fetching the beer: "rushing the growler." It became such a common practice that many saloon keepers installed a special service window called the "family entrance" which allowed women and children to avoid walking through the saloon to the bar.

This trend died out during Prohibition and did not return until the craft beer craze brought it back into vogue. Since my trip to New York City, growlers have arrived in British Columbia, big time, although they have been adopted in some communities more readily than others. They are just beginning to catch on in Vancouver, for instance, while Victoria has a thriving growler scene, with two brewpubs and every brewery except one participating. Happily, everyone will fill growlers from other breweries without complaint, though many growler enthusiasts end up buying more than one—even going so far as to collect them. Okay, I'll admit I have six already.

When Tofino Brewing opened in 2011, part of their business plan was connected to marketing growlers as good environmental choices for locals, trying to tap into the green-minded citizenry. It turns out they were overwhelmed by demand and now base most of their business on filling growlers at the brewery. Townsite Brewing in Powell River and Hoyne Brewing in Victoria each followed Tofino's lead when they opened in 2012 and both now do brisk business with the big brown jugs. Other breweries all around B.C. have opened growler stations, too, including Fernie Brewing, Cannery in Penticton, Arrowhead in Invermere, the Barley Station Brew Pub in Salmon Arm, the Noble Pig Brewhouse in Kamloops, Parallel 49 and Powell Street Craft Brewery in Vancouver, Bridge Brewing in North Vancouver, and others, I'm sure. Vancouver's Brassneck Brewery, slated to open in 2013, will be a growler-focused storefront that features a wide range of rotating taps and a choice of growler sizes to fill.

The scene in Victoria is particularly dynamic since there is so much variety. I was happy to find Hoyne's seasonal Wolf Vine Wet-Hopped Pale Ale available for growler fills when it came out, and Phillips Brewing, which has six growler taps available every day except Sunday, often makes one of its unusual or seasonal brews available. I check their website to see what's on tap—then it's simply a matter of tossing an empty growler in the back of my son's bike trailer—with him in his seat up front—and minutes later we're "rushing the growler."

www.phillipsbeer.com
250-380-1912
2010 Government Street, Victoria
E-MAIL info@phillipsbeer.com
TWITTER @phillipsbeer

Phillips Brewing

|||||||||||||||||||||||||||||||||||||||||||||

LIFT A GLASS to the legend of Matt Phillips.

After working at a few different breweries, including Whistler Brewing and Spinnakers, Phillips decided he wanted to start up his own operation. All the banks and credit unions turned down his loan applications, but, undeterred, he filled out every credit card application he could find and used that capital to fund his start-up. He lived in the brewery, showering at a nearby gym, and began brewing in earnest.

The first few years were precarious financially, and Phillips had to do everything himself. He even had to move his brewery when a ruptured tank resulted in a flood of Phoenix Lager (named in honour of the Victoria-Phoenix Brewery from a century earlier), which greatly displeased his landlord. Slowly but surely, though, his reputation grew, and so did his beer sales.

With growth came other challenges, including one from within the province's beer community. His flagship beer was Blue Truck Ale, named after the blue-painted milk truck he used to deliver his beer all over B.C., but Red Truck Brewing, part of the Mark James Group, didn't like the similarity to their brand. Phillips changed his beer's name to Blue Buck and kept on trucking.

Tap List

BLUE BUCK ALE
5% ABV
Phillips' flagship beer: a solid, malt-forward pale ale that you can find on tap almost everywhere on Vancouver Island.

DOUBLE DRAGON IMPERIAL RED ALE (seasonal)
8.2% ABV
This is one of my favourite seasonal brews from Phillips: rich and malty, with a dose of hop bitterness to balance it.

RASPBERRY WHEAT (seasonal)
5% ABV
One of Phillips' original brews, this refreshing beer brewed with B.C. raspberries is perfect for a summer patio.

AMNESIAC DOUBLE IPA
8.5% ABV
I love this beer. I think. Wait a sec, I forget. No, I do, really. It's big, strong and hoppy, but so well balanced.

By 2008, Phillips needed to expand. He found an ideal space on Government Street in the heart of Victoria's Design District, just a few blocks from Vancouver Island Brewery and close enough to the Inner Harbour to be accessible by foot for beer-loving tourists (see "Victoria's Beer Mile" on page 56). The brewery has a storefront for beer and T-shirt sales, as well as a very popular growler filling station. With five beers available for growler fills on a rotating basis, I keep my eye on their website for the occasions when an unusual seasonal style appears on the list: perhaps one of their Grow-Hop IPA series, which features a single hop such as Amarillo, Centennial or Cascade—or sometimes even their excellent Hoperation Tripel Cross Belgian IPA or Amnesiac Double IPA.

Phillips Brewing is one of the B.C. craft beer industry's big success stories. From those early days of overdrawn credit cards to the domination of Blue Buck Ale throughout Vancouver Island, where Lucky Lager once reigned, it's a tale worth celebrating. Best thing is it's based on great beer, consistently brewed without skimping or cheating. And it's all true. If you think I'm telling tales, take a brewery tour (Wednesday and Thursday afternoons at 4:00 PM) where you will see the old blue truck, now retired, in the back lot.

....

Facts & Figures

OPENED ‣ *2001* ✪ **STYLES PRODUCED** ‣ *12 + innumerable seasonals* ✪ **WHERE TO BUY** ‣ *Liquor stores throughout B.C.* ✪ **ON TAP** ‣ *All over Vancouver Island and in select spots in Greater Vancouver* ✪ **GROWLERS** ‣ *Yes*

www.spinnakers.com
250-386-2739
308 Catherine Street, Victoria
E-MAIL spinnakers@spinnakers.com
TWITTER @spinnakers

Spinnakers Gastro Brewpub

Tap List

MITCHELL'S EXTRA SPECIAL BITTER

5.2% ABV | 40 IBU

The original and still perhaps the best ESB in B.C. Michael Jackson, the celebrated British beer writer, called it "beautifully balanced."

LION'S HEAD CASCADIA DARK ALE

6.5% ABV | 55 IBU

A leader in the CDA style category: dark, malty and hoppy. Just delicious.

NORTHWEST ALE

6.2% ABV | 85 IBU

One of my favourite B.C. beers, this hop bomb is balanced with a strong malt foundation.

TSARIST IMPERIAL STOUT

7.75% ABV | 16 IBU

Stout lovers rejoice over this sweet black crude, brewed in the style of English stouts that were shipped to St. Petersburg before the Russian Revolution.

||||||||||||||||||||||||||||||||||||||||||||||||

WHEN ARCHITECT PAUL HADFIELD and two of his friends decided they wanted to open a brewpub on the shores of Victoria's Inner Harbour, it was illegal to do so in Canada. It was 1982, and although the opening of Horseshoe Bay Brewing that year had already marked the advent of the microbrewing movement in Canada, the brewpub concept, where beer is produced and sold within the same premises, was not allowed. The Horseshoe Bay brewery had to be physically separated from the Troller Pub where its beer was sold.

But Hadfield and his partners went ahead with their plans, lobbying the government hard, and a year and a half later, in May 1984, just two months after legislation was changed to allow for brewpubs, Spinnakers opened its doors and began pouring pints of hand-crafted, British-style beer. What a revolutionary concept!*

John Mitchell, one of the co-founders of Horseshoe Bay, came on board as a partner and was Spinnakers' original brewmaster, creating three signature brews to open the pub that are still regulars on the tap list today: Mitchell's Extra Special Bitter, Mt. Tolmie Dark and Empress Stout. He stayed around to brew the first forty batches there before moving on to other pursuits.

Hadfield became Spinnakers' publican in 1986, and under his guidance the brewpub has expanded considerably. It now boasts a nine-room guest house and a harbourside restaurant with a top-notch West Coast menu featuring locally sourced produce, meat, cheese and seafood. They also bottle their own malt vinegars and mineral water (from an aquifer 225 feet below the building), make their own chocolate truffles by hand and bake artisan breads and desserts on site. In 2004, as part of its twentieth anniversary, it was re-branded Spinnakers Gastro Brewpub to reflect its diverse offerings. And now, plans are in the works to open a bigger production brewery as part of the Roundhouse development across from the original brewpub and a Spinnakers outlet at the Victoria International Airport.

Most importantly, though, they haven't forgotten the original point: beer. Spinnakers' brews are some of the best you'll taste anywhere. You can choose one of four cask-conditioned beers poured at cellar temperature—pulled through classic English beer engines at the bar and served in proper pint glasses—or several other colder styles on draft.

Best time to visit? Any time is good, but each weekday at 4:00 PM is the Dog Watch when they tap a fresh cask right at the bar. And if Paul Hadfield is around, as he often is, ask him about the early days. You might just find you're still chatting with him at closing time.

* Looking back at those archaic laws that had to be changed for brewpubs to be allowed, maybe the politicians were right to be so strict. After all, Spinnakers did cause a revolution.

....
Facts & Figures

OPENED ▸ *1984* ✪ **STYLES PRODUCED ▸** *10 + seasonals* ✪ **WHERE TO BUY ▸** *At the brewpub and in private liquor stores in Victoria and Vancouver* ✪ **ON TAP ▸** *The brewpub and at the Lion's Head Pub in Robson* ✪ **GROWLERS ▸** *Yes*

www.swanshotel.com/brew-pub
250-361-3310
506 Pandora Avenue, Victoria
E-MAIL brewery@swanshotel.com

Swans Brewpub

IIIIIIIIIIIIIIIIIIIIIIIIIIIIIIIIIIIIIIIIIIIIII

IN THE FALL OF 1991, I moved five thousand kilometres from southern Ontario to Victoria, about as far as I could go and still stay in Canada. I had no job lined up, and not much money saved, but I was twenty-one and had my entire life ahead of me. My brother Pete and I rented a little house right across from the terminus of a brand-new walkway along the Inner Harbour that connected with downtown Victoria. It became our regular route—following the meandering path, we could be downtown in fifteen minutes by bike or rollerblades, or forty-five minutes by foot.

We quickly discovered Spinnakers, conveniently located on the walkway midway between our home and downtown. Not surprisingly, Pete and I often stopped there for a "halfway pint" or two. But Spinnakers wasn't the only stop on our own private ale trail—at the downtown end sat Swans, a beautifully renovated hotel and brewpub that became our default evening spot because of the regular live music on offer (and the fact that Spinnakers closes at 10:30 PM due to neighbourhood bylaws).

My brother and I were hooked instantly by the big main bar room with its high

Tap List

APPLETON BROWN ALE
5% ABV
My go-to beer during my first year in Victoria twenty years ago, this is as good as ever.

BUCKERFIELD'S BITTER
5% ABV
A creamy, malty and bitter ESB—in other words, perfect.

COCONUT PORTER (seasonal)
5.5% ABV
A gold medal winner at the Canadian Brewing Awards. Creamy with a light coconut aftertaste.

EXTRA IPA
6.8% ABV
This West Coast IPA is hoppy and strong, somewhere between a standard and imperial IPA, hence an "extra."

ceilings, bricks and beams, and original artwork everywhere. Until the Canoe Brewpub opened just down the street, I thought Swans was the best place to drink a beer in B.C. simply based on the room itself. Owner Michael Williams had renovated the building from the feed warehouse it was when he bought it, transforming it into a gorgeous hotel with a brewery and pub on the bottom. An avid art collector, much of his collection resides in the pub and hotel rooms upstairs. When he died in 2000, he bequeathed the entire place to the University of Victoria, and happily those smart people have not changed a thing since then.

Of course, the beer had to be good to keep me coming, and it still is. Its brewery was set up in 1989 by Frank Appleton, who, together with John Mitchell, helped kick-start the craft brewing movement in B.C. when they built Horseshoe Bay Brewing in 1982. He got things started and then hired a young graduate student named Sean Hoyne to be the first full-time brewer. Since 2003, the brewer has been Andrew Tessier, who grew up in Victoria. Tessier worked on the mainland at Backwoods Brewing (now Dead Frog) and R&B Brewing before becoming the brewmaster at Propeller Brewing in Halifax in 2001. He jumped at the opportunity to come home to Victoria when the job came open at Swans two years later.

My brother and I only lived in that house for a year. He moved to Vancouver and then back to Toronto, poor guy. Recently, Pete brought his family out west for a visit, and he and I headed down to Swans one evening. When the waitress came by to take our order, the words just rolled off my tongue as if twenty years had never passed.

"An Appleton Brown Ale and a Buckerfield's Bitter, please."

....
Facts & Figures

OPENED ‣ *1989* ✪ **STYLES PRODUCED** ‣ *9 + seasonals* ✪ **WHERE TO BUY** ‣ *In bottles from their neighbouring store, or in private liquor stores in Victoria and Vancouver* ✪ **ON TAP** ‣ *The brewpub* ✪ **GROWLERS** ‣ *No*

VICTORIA'S
BEER MILE

....

AS I WAS working on this book, I moved back to Victoria after twelve years away, and some old friends threw me a great welcome back party—they took me on a tour of what one them dubbed "the Beer Mile." This mile-long loop (1.6 kilometres just doesn't roll off the tongue so we'll put aside metric usage for now) features four distinct brewpubs whose origins span three decades of the craft brewing movement in B.C.

Begin this counter-clockwise route at the Canoe Brewpub (450 Swift Street), nestled in a beautiful spot right down on the water below the Johnson Street Bridge, making it the perfect place to debate the relative merits of replacing or refurbishing that historic structure over a pint.

There is a Victoria Harbour Ferry (www.victoriaharbour ferry.com) stop right outside the Canoe—a $5 ride will get you to your next stop on the Beer Mile and also give you a unique perspective on the industrial waterfront of Victoria where new housing and retail developments are blossoming among shipyards, cement factories and other traditional businesses. Call ahead of time (250-514-9794) to request a boat to take you one stop north to Point Ellice Historic House, just beyond the Point Ellice Bridge (which locals just call the Bay Street Bridge). From there it's a short walk to the newest member of Victoria's brewpub club, the Moon Under Water (350 Bay Street).

Heading west from the Moon Under Water across the Point Ellice Bridge you now have to complete the longest leg of this quest for beer: about half a mile following Bay Street to Catherine Street and then down to the shore of the Inner Harbour. There you will find Spinnakers (308 Catherine Street), which was Canada's first modern-day brewpub when it opened in 1984.

After Spinnakers, you're on the home stretch. The final leg of the Beer Mile is a ten-minute walk (hopefully not a stumble) back to downtown along the Songhees Walkway, which follows the shoreline of the Inner Harbour with camera-worthy views of the downtown waterfront, the Empress Hotel and the provincial Parliament Buildings. Across the Blue Bridge is Swans (506 Pandora Avenue), which opened in 1989 in a heritage building with comfortable hotel rooms upstairs. Swans is a great place to finish the Beer Mile since the pub offers live music every night of the week.

If you want to stretch the Beer Mile out over a couple of days, stay at Swans or Spinnakers and visit some of the other craft breweries nearby. Hoyne Brewing and the Driftwood Brewery are only a block away from the Moon Under Water at the corner of Hillside Avenue and Bridge Street, but neither offers official tours. Still, you might be able to arrange an informal visit at one or the other, and both do have growler stations. Phillips Brewing (2010 Government Street) and Vancouver Island Brewery (2330 Government Street) in the Design District just a few of blocks from Swans and the Canoe offer tours (check their websites for tour dates), and both have storefronts with growler filling stations. Lighthouse Brewing, the furthest afield, but still just a twenty-minute detour from this loop, also opened a tasting room and growler station as part of their expanded brewery in early 2013.

www.vanislandbrewery.com
250-361-0005
2330 Government Street, Victoria
E-MAIL info@vanislandbrewery.com
TWITTER @vanislebrewery

Vancouver Island Brewery

||||||||||||||||||||||||||||||||||||||||||||

Tap List

PIPER'S PALE ALE

5% ABV | 38 IBU

A multiple award winner, including gold medals at the 2009 and 2010 World Beer Championships.

HERMANN'S DARK LAGER

5.5% ABV | 30 IBU

Named for the brewery's original Bavarian brewmaster, this is an excellent example of the German Dunkel style.

FLYING TANKER WHITE IPA (seasonal)

6.8% ABV | 65 IBU

A complex hybrid that marries the Northwest IPA style with a spicy Belgian yeast.

HERMANNATOR ICE BOCK (seasonal)

9.5% ABV | 35 IBU

Celebrating its twenty-fifth anniversary in 2013, this unusual German Eisbock is cold-aged for over three months.

VANCOUVER ISLAND BREWERY was founded in 1984 as Island Pacific Brewing, the same year as Spinnakers Brewpub and Granville Island Brewing in Vancouver, making it one of B.C.'s original microbreweries (the name was changed in 1991). As Victoria's first stand-alone craft brewery, it has long been one of the industry leaders in the beer-drenched provincial capital. VIB has remained popular and stable—as a respected elder of sorts—while several new young bucks, first Lighthouse, then Phillips, Driftwood and Hoyne, appeared on the scene.

The thing with being a grizzled old veteran in the beer industry is that many craft beer lovers, especially younger ones, are interested in finding new styles and brands, checking off beers on their lists and seeking out that next great hop bomb. VIB's beers have been fine forever, but apart from the Hermannator Ice Bock, an annual winter seasonal that goes back twenty-five years itself, there wasn't anything in their lineup that made the average beer geek's heart flutter. It had the respect of many B.C. beer lovers, but didn't inspire the sort of excited devotion reserved for the newer, edgier breweries.

But the brewery started to feel the love after the release of its first specialty bomber, Flying Tanker White IPA, in 2012. It was a very interesting beer and it immediately grabbed the attention of a lot of the province's beer lovers. VIB followed it up in the autumn with a delicious Oktoberfest-style beer called Iron Plow Harvest Märzen. Early in 2013, they released Absolute Darkness India Dark Ale, and rumours were swirling as this book was going to press about the prospect of the addition of a new hoppy IPA to the regular lineup. Now that would make things really interesting.

Vancouver Island Brewery has one of the largest brewing facilities among the microbreweries in B.C., definitely worth visiting on a tour (Friday and Saturday afternoons). A new storefront tasting bar and growler station was another smart addition in 2012.

Facts & Figures

OPENED › *1984* ✿ **STYLES PRODUCED ›** *6 + seasonals* ✿ **WHERE TO BUY ›** *Liquor stores throughout B.C.* ✿ **ON TAP ›** *Throughout Vancouver Island* ✿ **GROWLERS ›** *Yes*

TAPHOUSES

Victoria

•••••••••••••••••••••••

HERE ARE MY top five places to check out the local beer scene.

Beagle Pub
301 Cook Street
A great pub with a long tap list in Cook Street Village. The Beagle hosts cask nights and other beer events on a regular basis.

Clive's Classic Lounge
740 Burdett Avenue
This comfy hotel bar offers excellent craft beer selections from Europe and the UK, with local beer available by the bottle only.

Christie's Carriage House
1739 Fort Street
This popular pub on the edge of Oak Bay is the only place I've found in Victoria that serves Crannóg's legendary Back Hand of God Stout along with most of the local brews.

Garrick's Head Pub
1140 Government Street
Victoria's best taphouse, this Bastion Square pub was renovated late in 2012 and now boasts a long bar with forty-four taps—twenty-two local brews and the rest from elsewhere.

Yates Street Tap House
759 Yates Street
With forty taps, this is part of what I hope will be a wave of new multi-tap pubs in Victoria.

BOTTLE SHOPS
Victoria

•••••••••••••••••••••••

VICTORIA HAS a wide assortment of private liquor stores where you can find local favourites or interesting craft beer from elsewhere.

Cascadia Liquor
4-2631 Quadra Street

Cask & Keg
852 Esquimalt Road

Cook Street Village Liquor
109-230 Cook Street
(around back)

Hillside Liquor Store
3201 Shelbourne Street

Liquor Express (Four locations)
12-1153 Esquimalt Road
3170 Tillicum Road
930 View Street
759 Yates Street

Liquor Plus
2915 Douglas Street

**Spinnakers Spirit Merchants
(Two locations)**
130-176 Wilson Street
425 Simcoe Street

The Strath
919 Douglas Street

BEST BEERS

Victoria

. . . .

Driftwood Brewery Fat Tug IPA
One of the best IPAS *anywhere*, not just in B.C.; if you could drink just one beer in B.C., this is it.

Hoyne Brewing Hoyner Pilsner
This is exactly what I remember drinking in Prague and Plzen on my trip to the Czech Republic ten years ago.

Lighthouse Brewing Siren Red Ale
Although this red bombshell of a beer caught my attention with its racy label, I was hooked by its even more enticing flavour.

Phillips Amnesiac Double IPA
Such a good beer for such a low price; makes me wonder why so many other bombers cost $3 or $4 more.

Spinnakers Northwest Ale
If you wanted to create a special category for "Northwest Ales," this would be the prototypical example.

THE ISLANDS & THE SUNSHINE COAST

AT THE BREWERY	DRAFT	FOOD	GROWLERS	BOTTLE SALES	TOURS	BEDS
Craig Street Brew Pub	★	★	★			
Longwood Brewpub	★	★	★	★	★	
Salt Spring Island Ales	★		★	★	★	
Tofino Brewing			★	★	★	
Townsite Brewing			★	★	★	
Wolf Brewing				★		

ISLAND ALE TRAIL

．．．．．．．．．．．．．．．．．．．．．．．

NOTORIOUSLY INDEPENDENT, wanting as little as possible to do with the Mainland, Vancouver Islanders are a loyal breed when it comes to beer. For the latter half of the twentieth century, that loyalty was to Lucky Lager, a brand that was brewed in Victoria by Labatt from 1958 to 1981. After Labatt demolished its historic brewery in 1982 (see "From Swan Lake to Spring Ridge" on page 34), Lucky was mainly brewed in Edmonton and sometimes in the Kokanee plant in Creston, but it continued to be most Islanders' beer of choice even as the craft beer revolution began bringing new and interesting brands to the island. That devotion might have had something to do with the beer's packaging which still describes it as "Vancouver Island's Original," or maybe it was just stubbornness. Mass market beer drinkers do tend to stick to one beer, kind of like long-suffering sports fans. (Go Canucks go!)

Vancouver Island Brewery was founded in 1984 (originally as Island Pacific Brewing) with the Vancouver Island market as its target. That company has had some success in converting people away from Lucky, and currently they produce the Islander lager brand as a direct attempt to woo residents. And Phillips Brewing has also made inroads with their Blue Buck Ale and Phoenix Lager brands.

But most towns outside Victoria are still Lucky towns, with only a few exceptions. The arrival of Tofino Brewing has changed the vibe up on the remote west coast of the island, and now the sight of someone with a growler of Tuff Session Ale or Hoppin' Cretin IPA is as common as a surfboard up there, dude. The same kind of success has been enjoyed by Townsite Brewing, the new brewery in Powell River over on the Sunshine Coast across from Comox.

It seems like the trick for these small, remote towns is "build it and the locals will come." But Tofino and Powell River both have large contingents of urban ex-pats who brought a love of craft beer with them, which might be part of the reason for those communities' success stories. Unfortunately, the same can't be said for Comox's short-lived Surgenor Brewing, which closed after only a few years of operations. We'll have to see how Beachcomber Brewing, a new brewery planned for Gibsons, fares. I think the name alone will guarantee its success, as will its proximity to the Vancouver market only a short ferry ride away.

Nanaimo has a longer history of brewing, but apart from the Longwood Brewpub, there hasn't been a big success story there yet, something Wolf Brewing hopes to change. The Cowichan Valley, a popular food and wine lover's paradise, has a jewel of a brewpub in Duncan, along with some cideries that might interest craft beer lovers. Add Salt Spring Island Ales to the mix and you have a short but compelling Island Ale Trail.

www.craigstreet.ca
250-737-BEER (2337)
25 Craig Street, Duncan
E-MAIL csbrewery@shaw.ca

Craig Street Brewpub

Tap List

MT. PREVOST PORTER

5% ABV | 26 IBU

A smooth, dark porter with a great roasted malt character. Perfect on a cold, rainy day.

SUMMER WHEAT BEER (seasonal)

4.8% ABV | 22 IBU

An excellent Hefeweizen. Only available as a summer seasonal.

||||||||||||||||||||||||||||||||||||||||||||||

DUNCAN IS A small city about an hour north of Victoria and halfway to Nanaimo, making it the perfect pit stop on a road trip "up-Island," as the locals say. And the ideal place to take a break is the stylish and comfortable Craig Street Brewpub. It is the Cowichan Valley's first and only brewpub, with a regular lineup of pale ale, lager, porter and Irish ale on tap, along with diverse specialty brews.

After moving to Victoria from Saskatchewan in the early 1990s, Chris Gress learned how to brew in his own backyard while he worked as a server at a popular downtown restaurant. One night there was a particularly loud table at the restaurant, and when he overheard that the patrons were from Duncan, he joked that there was no good beer there. The table went silent, he remembers, and one of the people there told him that would be changing soon. These were the business partners who were opening Craig Street Brewpub. Chris applied for the brewer's job and has worked hard ever since to make Duncan a craft beer destination.

Facts & Figures

OPENED ▸ 2006 ❖ **STYLES PRODUCED ▸** 4 + seasonals ❖ **ON TAP ▸** The brewpub ❖ **GROWLERS ▸** Only Craig Street growlers

SCRUMPY, CYSER & CIDER

Apples Never
Tasted So Good

● ●

FOR AN IDEAL detour off the Island Ale Trail, I recommend visiting Vancouver Island's iconic cideries: Merridale and Sea Cider. Both produce exceptional ciders that rival what the province's best craft brewers do with barley and hops.

Merridale Ciderworks (1230 Merridale Road, Cobble Hill, 250-743-4293, www.merridalecider.com) offers traditional apple ciders as well as these unique brews: Scrumpy, a blend of ciders made from crab apples and sharp cider apples that runs to 11 per cent ABV; and Cyser, a 10 per cent ABV brew that involves fermenting local honey along with apple juice. Stop by for a tour and tasting, or even stay overnight in one of their well-appointed yurts. Be sure to check out their lineup of distilled products as well, including: Frizz (carbonated) vodka, and apple and blackberry brandies. Merridale has a lunch bistro and cider bar that are both open seven days a week.

Sea Cider Farm & Ciderhouse (2487 Mt. St. Michael Road, Saanichton, 250-544-4824, www.seacider.ca), located on the Saanich Peninsula close to Victoria, is another exciting cidery with interesting styles ranging from Flagship (6 per cent ABV) to Pomona and Cyser (both at 16 per cent ABV) and Pommeau (18 per cent ABV), a still, aperitif-style cider. Sea Cider is open year round for tastings and tours.

GET LOCAL

B.C.'s Craft Brewers use
Local Ingredients

....

USING LOCAL ingredients in brewing has been part of the craft beer movement since long before the terms "locavore" and "100-mile diet" entered the foodie lexicon, but there is no doubt that interest in local beers has grown in recent years. No true estate brewery exists in B.C., unfortunately, mainly because the climate here is not well suited to growing barley, but Crannóg Ales comes the closest with its farm brewery concept, and they do use their own hops exclusively.

Several other B.C. breweries are growing their own hops to use in some specialty batches—usually fresh-hopped beers brewed right after the harvest in the fall—including Salt Spring Island Ales, which grows them on a nearby farm, and Spinnakers, which has a hop yard in Sooke, about an hour from the brewpub. But generally, B.C.'s craft breweries are leaving the production of hops to the hop farmers.

On the grain side of things, while it is difficult to grow barley effectively in the damp, coastal climate, one Saanich farmer named Mike Doehnel has been working at it for a while and has had some success. Driftwood Brewery has been his main customer—they have used his hand-malted barley in several seasonal specialties, including: Sartori Harvest IPA, which also uses fresh hops from Chilliwack's Sartori Cedar Ranch; Cuvée d'Hiver, a saison it brewed in 2011; and Spring Rite Abbey Ale, which was also brewed in 2011.

Phillips Brewing has produced the most local beer yet: their 24-Mile Blueberry Pail Ale used Doehnel's malted barley along with hops from another Saanich farm and local blueberries.

Apart from hops and barley, some B.C. brewers source interesting local ingredients to add to their brews. Pumpkin beers, like fresh-hopped beers, are popular in the autumn, and most breweries try to find local sugar pumpkins for their brews. Berries are the most common local adjunct, including blueberries, blackberries, raspberries, strawberries and even huckleberries, which Fernie Brewing uses to produce its excellent What the Huck Huckleberry Wheat beer all year round. Cherries, peaches and apricots also make an appearance in beers, especially from Okanagan breweries, which certainly makes sense given the stone-fruit orchards there.

Tofino Brewing caught some attention at the Central City Summer Cask Festival in 2011 with its cask of IPA flavoured with locally harvested spruce tips. Phillips also tried adding spruce tips to an ale in 2012 with not quite as much success. Maybe the IPA was able to "handle" the spruce flavour better than a more basic ale—in the Phillips brew it was a bit overwhelming.

www.longwoodbrewpub.com
250-729-8225
5775 Turner Road, Nanaimo
E-MAIL reservations@
longwoodbrewpub.com
www.longwoodbeer.com

Longwood Brewpub

||||||||||||||||||||||||||||||||||||||||||||||

FOR YEARS, the Longwood Brewpub has been an oasis in the craft beer desert of central Vancouver Island. Heck, when it opened in 1999, there was nowhere else north of Victoria. The centrepiece of the Longwood Station plaza, this brewpub is a gorgeous building from the outside, and the inside is even better. The ground floor and patio has more of a restaurant feel while the atmosphere downstairs is more of a pub with a big field-stone fireplace and dark wood throughout. It is decidedly not a sports bar—although there are small TVs, the sound is intentionally never cranked up. Rather, this is the sort of place to go to enjoy a pint and a conversation with friends, just like a traditional English pub.

Like Spinnakers and Swans, the brewpub has four English-style draught engines pulling cellar-conditioned beer—appropriate styles such as ESB, Irish red ale, Scotch ale and imperial stout. They also serve continental styles at colder draft temperatures, including a very good Czech Pilsner and Dunkelweizen. They try to use locally grown hops from nearby Port Alberni and Gabriola Island whenever they can, often in cask-conditioned beers which are served

Tap List

**EXTRA
SPECIAL BITTER**
6% ABV
John Mitchell's
original Spinnakers
recipe. Delicious.

INDIA PALE ALE
6.8% ABV
A good English-style IPA.

DUNKELWEIZEN
5.5% ABV
A very nice, light-bodied,
dark-coloured German
wheat beer.

SCOTTISH ALE (seasonal)
6.5% ABV
A very creamy, well-
rounded, malty ale.

from the bar on Firkin Fridays from 3:30 PM on. This is when Nanaimo's beer geeks make an appearance.

After working his way up to head brewer at Spinnakers in the early 1990s, Barry Ladell became a brewery consultant and was hired to design the Longwood. Excited by the prospect, he bought in as a partner, became its first brewer and stuck around as publican until 2012 when he left for other pursuits. Harley Smith had been the main brewer there for a decade and took over the title as well after Ladell's departure. I visited when Ladell was still in charge and he described the history and future plans of the place with great passion and pride: one of his dreams, that the brewpub open a separate production brewery, was finally achieved early in 2013.

Ladell wasn't a fan of hoppy beers—"I don't like Homeland Security and I don't like American IPA," he said with a wry chuckle—so it will be interesting to see if some hoppier styles begin appearing on the menu following his departure.

As part of launching their new production brewery, Longwood rebranded its lineup of bottled beers with stylish, new labels and names. Harley Smith says the recipes of the beers inside are much the same as they are at the brewpub, and added that he will also be releasing seasonal beers in the 650 ml bomber format in the future.

....
Facts & Figures

OPENED › *1999* ✸ **STYLES PRODUCED** › *6 + seasonals* ✸ **WHERE TO BUY** › *In growlers or bottles from the brewpub* ✸ **ON TAP** › *The brewpub* ✸ **GROWLERS** › *Yes*

www.gulfislandsbrewery.com
250-653-2383 · 1-866-353-2383
270 Furness Road, Salt Spring Island
E-MAIL info@gulfislandsbrewery.com
TWITTER @SaltSpringAles

Salt Spring Island Ales (Gulf Islands Brewery)

Tap List

**EXTRA
SPECIAL BITTER**
5.5% ABV
A great, flavourful ESB made with whole-cone hops and organic malts.

DRY PORTER
5.5% ABV
A light-to-medium-bodied porter with a great chocolate and roasted malt character.

HEATHER ALE
5% ABV
Infused with heather flowers from the world-famous Butchart Gardens, this ancient style dates back to 2000 BC.

**SPRING FEVER
GRUIT** (seasonal)
5% ABV
This ancient ale style is brewed entirely with a variety of wild herbs, roots and spices—and no hops at all.

THE SOUTHERN GULF ISLANDS between Victoria and Vancouver in the Salish Sea/Georgia Strait are among the most picturesque places in beautiful British Columbia. If I could afford it, I'd keep a cabin on one for sure; I even imagine I could live there, at least part-time—while writing a book perhaps— if not for the paucity of craft beer to be found. Of all the islands—Pender, Mayne, Galiano, Saturna and Salt Spring—only one boasts a brewery. Each of these islands deserves to be home to an idyllic brewpub, and Salt Spring is big enough to have a few.

Yet, up until recently, even Salt Spring's brewery had no public storefront despite its ideal location right off the main road between the ferry dock and Ganges, the main town on the island. If all goes according to plan, however, the brewery will be opening a tasting room and a pair of rustic cabins for rent by the time this book is published, and I can just imagine the effect a sign reading "Turn left for fresh craft beer" will have on the many tourists who drive that route each year. They might have to install a traffic light.

The brewery was founded as Gulf Islands Brewery in 1998 by Bob Ellison and Murray

Hunter, who had run an all-grain brew-on-premises operation called Murray's Brewplace on Salt Spring before that. In 2009, "Uncle Bob" sold his interest in the company to family friends Neil Cooke-Dallin and Becky Julseth, who live in Victoria, and they took over the management of the brewery with Hunter staying on as brewmaster. Neil and Becky had no previous experience with brewing, but they have applied their love of fine local food and craft beer, and their rebranding of the bottled products has increased marketability significantly.

Based in a converted barn on a fourteen-acre lot at the base of Mount Bruce, the tallest peak on Salt Spring Island, the brewery uses water from a naturally flowing spring on the mountainside above, and produces and packages its beer entirely on the island. In 2009, they planted hops in a nearby farm field, and each year they pick the crop as part of a harvest festival, using the hops for a special fresh-hopped beer. They also use local ingredients such as honey and heather in their beers, and have pioneered the production of an ancient beer style called Gruit that uses no hops at all.

While you can find their beers on tap in a variety of restaurants and pubs in Victoria, I highly recommend a visit to the idyllic island paradise itself.

Facts & Figures

OPENED ‣ *1998* ○ **STYLES PRODUCED** ‣ *5 + seasonals* ○ **WHERE TO BUY** ‣ *The brewery, or in liquor stores in Vancouver and on Salt Spring and Vancouver Island* ○ **ON TAP** ‣ *Victoria and on Salt Spring Island* ○ **GROWLERS** ‣ *Yes*

www.tofinobrewingco.com
250-725-2899
681 Industrial Way, Tofino
E-MAIL info@tofinobrewingco.com
TWITTER @tofinobrewco

Tofino Brewing

||||||||||||||||||||||||||||||||||||||||||||

Tap List

TUFF SESSION ALE
5% ABV | 25 IBU

A bright, copper-coloured pale ale with a toasty malt base balanced with West Coast hops.

HOPPIN' CRETIN IPA
7% ABV | 60 IBU

A tawny, heartily hopped, West Coast IPA that gives off an aromatic bouquet of citrus and mango.

FOGUST
WHEAT ALE (seasonal)
4.5% ABV | 10 IBU

A German-style, unfiltered Hefeweizen that is light and hazy with subtle notes of banana and clove up front.

DAWN PATROL COFFEE
PORTER (seasonal)
6.5% ABV | 20 IBU

The potent smoky bitterness of roasted coffee blends perfectly with the sweet malt flavours of this dark elixir.

WHEN TOFINO BREWING opened its doors in the spring of 2011, it was like a novice surfer trying to stand up on a longboard for the very first time. As any newbie will admit, you splash into the water much more often than you manage to stay on your feet, and the frigid Pacific Ocean waters off the west coast of Vancouver Island make the task even more challenging.

Similarly, the fledgling brewery's trio of owners—all locals themselves—figured they'd have to work at winning people over one by one, converting them from long-held connections to other brands. So, in step with the community's strong interest in environmentalism, they decided to start off by selling refillable growlers. The brewery's first batch of three hundred growlers, which they thought would last them a month, sold out within a week of opening. An emergency order of six hundred more was gone in another week so they quickly ordered another thousand. They even stopped selling the jugs to tourists, recognizing that the local community had to be their focus.

"We had a growler for every man, woman and child in Tofino," quipped brewer Dave Woodward, who moved there from

Vancouver to craft the beer—true, considering the town's year-round population is about 1,650. Co-owner Chris Neufeld added that they had to change their business plan, capping keg sales to allow for the unexpected popularity of the growlers, which accounted for more than half of their business within a few months of opening. Indeed, when I visited the brewery in November 2011, there was a steady stream of customers stopping by on a Thursday evening to refill their growlers with some Tuff Session Ale, Hoppin' Cretin IPA or a special seasonal brew.

As much as possible, Tofino Brewing tries to access the local agricultural community for ingredients, including wild berries, hops from a Port Alberni farm and spruce tips harvested from the surrounding forest in the spring. They also work with local business partners, such as Shelter Restaurant, where all their beers are featured, and Tofino Roasting, a coffee company across the street that created a custom roast for the brewery's Dawn Patrol Coffee Porter.

The brewery installed a bottling line in late 2012, which will allow them to begin offering their beer in 650 mL bombers; this will certainly help them expand their sales to bigger markets in Victoria and Vancouver.

As B.C. destinations go, it doesn't get much better than Tofino, so Tofino Brewing is well worth a visit. While you're there, maybe you can try to catch a wave, dude.

Facts & Figures

OPENED ‣ *2011* ✪ **STYLES PRODUCED** ‣ *5 + seasonals* ✪ **WHERE TO BUY** ‣ *The brewery or private liquor stores in Vancouver and Victoria.* ✪ **ON TAP** ‣ *Tofino, Victoria and Vancouver* ✪ **GROWLERS** ‣ *Yes*

www.townsitebrewing.com
604-483-2111
5824 Ash Avenue, Powell River
E-MAIL karen@townsitebrewing.com
TWITTER @townsitebrewing

Townsite Brewing

||||||||||||||||||||||||||||||||||||||||||||

IN POWELL RIVER, the past, present and future are interwoven in the very geography. Born as a mill town a century ago, the original townsite was built between 1910 and 1930 by the Powell River Paper Company according to a utopian planning philosophy called the Garden City movement that respected the humanity of industrial workers and their families first and foremost. The resulting grid of houses around and above the paper mill was recognized as a National Historic Site in 1995.

Tap List

ZUNGA GOLDEN BLONDE ALE
5% ABV | 25 IBU
Zunga is Powell River-ese for "rope swing over water." Dive into this refreshing blonde ale.

TIN HAT IPA
6% ABV | 55 IBU
A solid West Coast IPA with an aromatic hop nose and a great malt foundation.

POW TOWN PORTER
6% ABV | 35 IBU
A rich, creamy porter with a great roasted malt character. Ideal for a rainy evening in front of the fireplace.

SHINY PENNY (seasonal)
8.5% ABV | 80 IBU
This complex Belgian IPA is a potent marriage of brewer Cédric Dauchot's Belgian heritage and North American brewing sensibilities.

The Townsite neighbourhood features well-maintained heritage houses built in the Arts and Crafts style that can be had for a song compared to anything in Vancouver or Victoria. As a result, Townsite has become the destination for a wave of urban ex-pats fleeing the bustle and exorbitant real estate prices of Vancouver. Although it's a five-hour drive (including two ferries) back to the city, many of these "real estate refugees" recognize the benefits of Pow Town's affordability, and artsy, outdoorsy vibe.

Karen Skadsheim arrived in 2007 after a year of travelling abroad, intending to stay with her brother for a while before returning to urban life in North Vancouver. After a year passed, she had become so well connected in the community that she realized her future lay right there. The only thing missing for her was craft beer.

"This brewery is all about me and my needs," she explained with a laugh when I visited the brewery for their opening in March 2012. Rumours of new microbreweries opening on the Sunshine Coast came and went, and she and her friends often talked about the perfect building for such a brewery: an architectural treasure built by the federal government in 1939 to house the post and customs offices that had sat empty for a long time. One night, after a couple of beers, she e-mailed the address on the For Lease sign, saying she was looking into setting up a microbrewery in town and wondered what the rent would be. The owner loved the idea and formed a partnership with her to build the brewery.

After two years of planning and preparation, Townsite Brewing opened in April 2012 in typically Powell River fashion: with an eclectic parade that featured decorated goats and a bride and groom riding in a bicycle rickshaw carrying the first keg of beer in their laps. The brewery's launch was very successful—its first order of 550 growlers sold out in a month, and demand for refills pushed the brewery to open seven days a week by early summer.

As the Sunshine Coast's only brewery, Townsite was primarily aiming to convert the locals to its brews, but Skadsheim has been surprised by just how enthusiastic the response has been. Massive interest from beer lovers in Vancouver meant she had to figure out how to get shipments down the coast to the city she'd left behind. A big part of that success is due to the brewmaster she hired, Cédric Dauchot, who brings a Belgian brewing pedigree with him (see "From Belgium to B.C." on page 78).

Facts & Figures

OPENED ▸ *2012* ✪ **STYLES PRODUCED** ▸ *6 + seasonals* ✪
WHERE TO BUY ▸ *At the brewery and private stores in Vancouver and on the Sunshine Coast* ✪ **ON TAP** ▸ *Sunshine Coast and Vancouver* ✪ **GROWLERS** ▸ *Yes*

FROM BELGIUM
TO B.C.

Townsite Brewing's
Cédric Dauchot

•••••••••••••••••••••••

A KEY PART of Townsite Brewing's story is its brewer, Cédric Dauchot, the only Belgian-born-and-trained brewer in B.C.

Dauchot grew up just south of Brussels, close to France. He graduated from L'institut Meurice in Brussels in 2004 as a chemistry-biochemistry engineer with an emphasis on fermentation and the brewing industries. Most of his classmates ended up taking jobs with Belgian brewing empire Interbrew (now called Anheuser Busch-InBev), the world's largest brewer with 25 per cent of the global market share. His own experience there as a lab technician for a few months was enough to make him realize he did not want to go that route with his brewing career. Little did he know he'd end up about as far from that as one can get, both figuratively and physically.

After graduating, he took a job with the French chain Les 3 Brasseurs, which sent him to Montreal to set up several brewpubs in Quebec. During his four years there, he met and married a Canadian woman named Chloe Smith, who is a brewer herself. After learning everything there is to know about setting up breweries, they moved to her hometown of Saskatoon to try to open their own, the Shiny Penny Brewery, which they intended to be the first "gastronomic brewpub" in Saskatchewan. But after "chasing our own tail for a year and a half," Dauchot saw an advertisement for a head brewer in Powell River and decided to apply.

Townsite's founder, Karen Skadsheim, says she definitely wanted to hire him, but admits she was nervous about bringing this couple—who were about to have their first baby—all the way to the remote northern end of the Sunshine Coast, far from family and friends. She needn't have worried. As Dauchot explains in his accented but perfect English, "Saskatoon to Powell River is less far than Belgium to Canada."

It turned out to be the perfect fit. Cédric and Chloe love the Townsite neighbourhood's laid back, artistic vibe. Most importantly, Dauchot says, "I had the freedom to put the brewery together the way I wanted." Chloe also hopes to brew at Townsite—once baby Béatrix lets her.

With the recent surge in interest in Belgian styles in the craft beer world, Townsite is lucky to have its own resident expert, and he has already demonstrated his skills with a delicious Tripel he brewed for the Biercraft Belgian Showcase event during Vancouver Craft Beer Week in 2012, just a few months after Townsite Brewing opened. I had the pleasure of hanging out with Dauchot that night—we sampled various Belgian beers and he shared his memories of many of them. ("This is the one I used to drink when I was sixteen and getting into trouble," or, "This brewery is five minutes from my father's house.")

Late in the evening, the restaurant owner walked over with a small, unlabelled bottle and offered us each a tiny glassful. It was the fabled Westvleteren 12, a Trappist beer that is brewed exclusively by monks in Belgium and is incredibly hard to find. The monastery only sells the beer to the public once in a while, and usually with the proviso that it may not be resold. Of course, that only increases its value: I have seen a price tag of $25 for a single 250 mL bottle.

I was thrilled to try it at Biercraft, but Dauchot's reaction to it was priceless. "This should not be here!" he sputtered in shock, staring at the small glass in his hands as if it were liquid gold. He said we should find a quiet corner and insisted we warm the small glassful a little in our hands before sipping it. How was it? You'll have to try it yourself to find out. I want to keep that moment between Cédric and me.

www.wolfbrewingcompany.com
250-716-2739
2-940 Old Victoria Road, Nanaimo
E-MAIL info@wolfbrewingcompany.com

Wolf Brewing

Tap List

RANNOCH SCOTCH ALE
6% ABV | 30 IBU
This "wee heavy" is rich and malty with big caramel flavours. Delicious.

RED BRICK IPA
6% ABV
On the maltier side but with a substantial offering of hops, this is an English IPA with a bit of West Coast flair.

NANAIMO HAS NOT had much luck sustaining breweries. Only the Longwood Brewpub can be described as successful. One other operation, Fat Cat Brewery, struggled for more than a decade before it was sold and re-branded as Wolf Brewing in 2011. The new owners have been working at establishing new clients and developing new brews, and took a big step in the right direction by hiring Mike Pizzitelli, another young graduate of Heriot-Watt University. He has tweaked their previously unremarkable IPA just enough that it will grab a beer geek's attention without scaring away a more mainstream consumer. Some other specialty brews, including their potent and provocative Imperial Maple Stout, also demonstrate that they are on the right path.

I'm not quite howling at the moon yet, but I do think the future is bright for Wolf Brewing and the Nanaimo craft beer scene in general.

Facts & Figures

OPENED ▸ 2011 (originally Fat Cat Brewery, which opened in 2000)
✪ STYLES PRODUCED ▸ 5 ✪ WHERE TO BUY ▸ The brewery and in liquor stores on Vancouver Island ✪ GROWLERS ▸ No

BEST BEERS

The Islands
and the Sunshine Coast

••••••••••••••••••••••••

Craig Street Brewpub Summer Wheat Ale
A delicious Hefeweizen, perfect for a summer afternoon patio session.

Longwood Brewpub Scottish Ale
An excellent Scottish ale (not a peaty scotch ale): creamy, malty and delicious.

Salt Spring Island Ales ESB
Day trips to Salt Spring from Victoria will become regular occurrences for me once their tasting room and growler station opens.

Tofino Brewing Tuff Session Ale
If this book sells a million copies I think I will retire to Tofino and spend my royalties on growler fills of this bitchin' beer.

Townsite Brewing Pow Town Porter
Or maybe I'll retire to Powell River so I can sip this creamy porter gazing at the incredible sunset every night.

★ VANCOUVER ★

AT THE BREWERY	DRAFT	FOOD	GROWLERS	BOTTLE SALES	TOURS	BEDS
Coal Harbour Brewing					✪	
Dockside Brewing	✪	✪	✪		✪	✪
Granville Island Brewing	✪	✪		✪	✪	
Parallel 49 Brewing	✪		✪	✪		
Powell Street Craft Brewery			✪	✪	✪	
R&B Brewing			✪	✪		
Red Truck Beer					✪	
Steamworks Brewing	✪	✪	✪	✪		
Storm Brewing						
Yaletown Brewing	✪	✪	✪	✪	✪	

CRAFT BEER
CENTRAL

....

GASTOWN, VANCOUVER'S oldest neighbourhood, is named for
John "Gassy Jack" Deighton, the first European settler of the
community that would eventually become Vancouver. The story
goes that he arrived in a rowboat on September 30, 1867, with
his family, two chairs and a big barrel of whiskey. He told some
local sawmill workers they could have all the whiskey they
could drink in one sitting in exchange for building his bar. Thus,
his Globe Saloon was erected in one day and Gastown was born.

Deighton earned his "Gassy" nickname for the tall tales he
liked to spin, so who knows how much of this story is actually
true, but as far as city origins go, it's a pretty darn good one—
except, for my purposes, it's too bad it wasn't a barrel of beer.

Today, the Globe Saloon is long gone, but in the place where
it once was now stands a statue of Vancouver's unlikely founding father atop a giant whiskey barrel. Gastown is an eclectic
hybrid of souvenir stores, cutting-edge restaurants, dance
clubs and local fashion boutiques. But out on the very eastern
edge of Gastown, away from all that, is another saloon that
has played a seminal role in Vancouver's newest incarnation as
Craft Beer Central: the Alibi Room.

The Alibi Room is Vancouver's craft beer headquarters, the
one place to visit if you only have time for one stop—yes, even

over one of the city's excellent brewpubs. You'll find the best craft beer on tap there, both from B.C. and elsewhere, served by knowledgeable, beer-loving staff, along with excellent food and a comfortable, welcoming atmosphere. Behind the bar you might get to meet Nigel Springthorpe, decidedly less loquacious than the city's original saloon keeper, but a founding father of Vancouver's burgeoning craft beer scene nonetheless. (See "Nigel's Alibi" on page 112.)

Vancouver had little to offer craft beer lovers in the early days of B.C.'s craft beer revolution. After Granville Island Brewing opened in 1984, only Shaftebury opened in the city in the next decade. Fogg n' Suds, a chain started here in the 1980s, was an oasis for a time because of the diversity of beers on its menu. In the mid-'90s there was a brewpub boom with the opening of Yaletown Brewing, Steamworks, Dockside and Dix, but the only production breweries that opened during that decade were R&B and Storm, both pretty small affairs. And after Dix opened in 1998, no new breweries or brewpubs opened in the city until 2011. Most of the growth occurred in the suburbs where the lower cost of rent or real estate made the business of brewing more viable.

The Alibi Room's conversion to a craft beer focus in 2006 played a big role in waking up the city to craft beer. There were other contributing factors, too. Private liquor stores like Brewery Creek and Firefly began increasing their craft beer sections, which encouraged distributors to expand their portfolios. Cask-conditioned beer, which had been available once or twice a week in select pubs for a few years already, could now be found any night of the week, and seasonal multi-cask festivals became must-attend events. Other beer-focused pubs such as St. Augustine's followed, and the membership ranks of the Campaign for Real Ale (CAMRA) swelled. A younger generation of "foodies" turned to craft beer instead of wine, and food-pairing or brewmaster dinners followed. More and more women began showing up at craft beer events. And a new generation of brewers was ready for this surge in interest: skilled practitioners who answered the demand for new and more challenging styles head on.

Now that Vancouver has finally awakened to craft beer, the sleepy giant's thirst is nearly insatiable. Brewers say they can't brew enough to fill the demand. After more than a decade that saw no new breweries open in the city, suddenly three opened in 2012 alone (Coal Harbour, Parallel 49 and Powell Street) with a whopping five more planned for 2013, along with two more in nearby suburbs and big new production facilities planned for Red Truck Brewing and Steamworks.

Maybe it's time to start thinking about erecting another statue in Gastown.

STOP
THE PRESSES

······················

AS THIS BOOK neared publication, five new breweries were expected to open in Vancouver. Here is some basic information about each of them—as much as was available in July, 2013.

33 Acres Brewing | Opened: July
Brewer: Dave Varga (previously of Red Truck Beer)

15 West 8th Ave, Vancouver | (604) 367-8482
WEB: www.33acresbrewing.com | EMAIL: beer@33acresbrewing.com | TWITTER: @33Acres

Bomber Brewing | Projected Opening Date: November
Brewers: Blair Calibaba and Don Farion

1488 Adanac, Vancouver
WEB: www.bomberbrewing.com | EMAIL: info@bomberbrewing.com
TWITTER: @BomberBrewing

Brassneck Brewery | Projected Opening Date: August
Brewer: Conrad Gmoser (previously of Steamworks Brewing)

2148 Main Street, Vancouver
WEB: www.brassneck.ca | EMAIL: info@brassneck.ca | TWITTER: @Brassneckbrew

Dogwood Brewing | Projected Opening Date: Unknown
Brewer: Claire (Connolly) Wilson

WEB: www.dogwoodbrew.com | EMAIL: dogwood@dogwoodbrew.com
TWITTER: @DogwoodBrew

Main Street Brewing | Projected Opening Date: August
Brewer: Jack Bensley

263 East 7th Ave, Vancouver
WEB: www.mainstreetbrewingcompany.com | EMAIL: info@mainstreetbrewingcompany.com
TWITTER: @mainstreetbeer

www.coalharbourbrewing.com
604-215-7471
1967 Triumph Street, Vancouver
E-MAIL info@coalharbourbrewing.com
TWITTER @CoalHarBrew

Coal Harbour Brewing

Tap List

311 HELLES LAGER
5.25% ABV | 18 IBU
A genuine Munich-style lager. *Prosit!*

POWELL IPA
6.5% ABV | 66 IBU
A surprise gold medal winner at the 2012 Canadian Brewing Awards just weeks after it was first brewed.

TRIUMPH RYE ALE
5.25% ABV | 38 IBU
I love rye beers for their earthy malt bitterness—in this case perfectly paired against aromatic, bitter Northwest hops.

HUNTER'S MOON ROGGENWEIZEN
5.6% ABV | 33 IBU
A very unusual rye/wheat beer that is finished with *Brettanomyces*, a wild yeast that adds a bit of a musty, sour finish.

|||||||||||||||||||||||||||||||||||||||||||||

COAL HARBOUR BREWING opened quietly in early 2012 with a big plan to brew two specialty lagers, 311 Helles and Vancouver Vienna Lager. They added a rye ale almost as an afterthought. Well, it turns out the Triumph Rye Ale was their most popular brew, and when brewer Kevin Emms added the Powell IPA to the lineup later in spring, he was promptly rewarded with a gold medal at the Canadian Brewing Awards in the English IPA category. Not bad for a brand new beer from a brand new brewery.

Emms trained at the prestigious Heriot-Watt University in Edinburgh, so presumably he knows his stuff. His beer certainly reflects that. Early on, he had to deal with an unusually configured brewhouse with large fermentation tanks that were meant primarily for lagers and only one small fermenter for ales. Apparently the original tanks were too tall for the room so their conical bottoms were removed. But Emms figured out ways to work around that problem and now his ales are some of the most popular in the city. The lagers are nothing to scoff at either, although the local craft beer geek's taste for lagers is relatively undeveloped.

With Parallel 49 across the street, Storm Brewing nearby, and the Powell Street Craft Brewery around the corner, this East Vancouver neighbourhood is rapidly becoming the city's new brewing district, although they have competition in that regard with Main Street's growing Brewery Creek neighbourhood.

Facts & Figures

OPENED ⟩ *2012* ✪ **STYLES PRODUCED** ⟩ *4 + seasonals* ✪ **WHERE TO BUY** ⟩ *Liquor stores in the Lower Mainland and Greater Victoria* ✪ **ON TAP** ⟩ *Restaurants and pubs in Greater Vancouver* ✪ **GROWLERS** ⟩ *No*

www.docksidevancouver.com/
brewery
604-685-7070
1253 Johnston Street
(Granville Island), Vancouver
E-MAIL
info@docksidevancouver.com

Dockside Brewing Company

Tap List

**HAUPENTHAL
HEFEWEIZEN**

4.8% ABV

One of the more authentic
German wheat beers in
Vancouver.

RAILSPUR IPA

5.7% ABV

A well-balanced,
hop-forward IPA.

ORIGINALLY BUILT IN 1997 as part of the Granville Island Hotel, this brewpub shares its prime location right on the edge of False Creek with the Dockside Restaurant. Both pub and restaurant offer the same incredible patio with an amazing view of the glass towers of downtown Vancouver—it was perhaps *the* best patio in Vancouver until the two-level Tap & Barrel opened in the Olympic Village—making Dockside one of the best places to sip a beer in B.C. You can order the same beers in either the pub or restaurant, but the food menus are significantly different. The restaurant is excellent but on the pricier side of the scale, while the pub's fare is more than adequate—you can decide based on the size of your wallet.

As often is the case in brewpubs that cater to a wider tourist demographic, though, the beer is not particularly challenging, but it isn't bad either. It's a good, safe bet, and the brewpub puts the occasional cask-conditioned beer on as well.

Facts & Figures

OPENED ‣ *1997* ✿ **STYLES PRODUCED** ‣ *7 + seasonals* ✿
ON TAP ‣ *The brewpub* ✿ **GROWLERS** ‣ *Yes*

WHY ARE THERE
SO FEW BREWPUBS
IN VANCOUVER?

....

VANCOUVERITES HAVE fallen for craft beer, big time. Just check out the Alibi Room or St. Augustine's, beer-focused restaurants with ninety craft taps between them, which are usually full on any given night, and the numerous taphouses that have opened throughout the city. Nightly cask events somewhere in the city, brewmaster dinners, seasonal CAMRA events and the massive annual Vancouver Craft Beer Week all speak to craft beer's popularity here.

But when it comes to brewpubs, Vancouver's glass is far from overflowing. The closure of Dix in 2010 left the city with only three: Dockside Brewing, Steamworks Brew Pub and Yaletown Brewing. By comparison, craft beer's American mecca, Portland, Oregon, with a similar population, boasts more than thirty brewpubs. Even Victoria, with far fewer residents, has four, with a fifth on the way in nearby View Royal.

All of Vancouver's brewpubs came into being in the 1990s, with Dix the last to open in 1998, and no one has even applied to open a brewpub in the city since then. The partnership team behind St. Augustine's originally wanted to open it as a brewpub, but encountered resistance at City Hall beginning with their first request for information. Co-owner Anthony Frustagli says when the planning department's clerk asked, "What the hell is a brewpub?" he knew their initial dream was dead. They refocused on opening St. Augustine's instead, and then a production brewery, Parallel 49, a few years later.

Iain Hill, head brewer for the Mark James Group's chain of brewpubs, which currently includes Yaletown Brewing as well as two others in Surrey and Whistler (and once included Dix and another in North Vancouver), says the reason why there are so few in the city is "basically because you need a Liquor Primary."

The Liquor Primary licence, required by the provincial Liquor Control and Licensing Branch, entails a multi-step application process that includes posting site signage and distributing flyers to prospective neighbours, and could even include holding a public meeting to allow local residents to voice their concerns, or conducting a telephone survey. Each of these stages has a price tag: from $801 to a possible total of $4,327 depending on how many steps are required. The city's Licence Office considers a long list of factors before making a recommendation to Vancouver City Council, which ultimately approves or rejects the application. There is no set timeline for the application process, but it can often take a year or more.

As a result, Hill believes, it is nearly impossible for entrepreneurs who want to open a brewpub to do so in Vancouver. Since licence applications must be tied to specific locations, an applicant has to find a potential building to house the brewpub first. Unless this person owns a building or can afford to buy one, this will usually be under a lease arrangement. But the applicant must either be willing to pay rent for a year or more without any chance of seeing revenue, or find a landlord willing to wait that long before being paid. Add into that the high start-up costs inherent in brewpubs: the brewing equipment is expensive and often must be customized to fit the building.

And you cannot get around these rules by opening a brewery and a separate restaurant in the same building because of so-called "Tied Houses" rules. Early in 2013, the provincial government announced that "small- and medium-sized liquor manufacturers will be allowed up to three common ownership and business relationships with licensed establishments located off their manufacturing site." This does not change the brewpub situation, although it does, finally, allow a place like

St. Augustine's to sell Parallel 49 beer, something which wasn't allowed previously since both are owned by the same people.

The B.C. government also announced that "brewers and distillers now can apply to have an on-site consumption area such as a lounge, tasting room or event area." It was unclear at publication time how this application process would work—if it would require a brewery to apply for a Liquor Primary licence, for instance, and also, how zoning would come into play since breweries generally have to be in industrial zones where Liquor Primary licences are not normally allowed. However, if the process for breweries to open tasting rooms is simplified, and if they are allowed to serve basic food, too, this would open up the potential for a new hybrid between traditional brewpubs and microbreweries.

Regardless, Iain Hill argues that there is an immediate solution, and it's simple: "Why not allow a brewpub to open under a Food Primary licence?" As the name suggests, Food Primary licences are meant for restaurants with a food focus, and these licences are much easier to obtain since they do not require city council approval. They usually only take about two months and are mostly just a rubber-stamp procedure. But this would require a change in policy at the provincial level, not at Vancouver City Hall.

I think the solution lies in creating a new category specifically designed for brewpubs that takes into consideration the unique challenges those businesses face. With the huge potential in growth for brewpubs in Vancouver and around the province, it just makes sense.

www.gib.ca
604-687-2739
1441 Cartwright Street, Vancouver
E-MAIL info@gib.ca
TWITTER @itsgoodtobehere

Granville Island Brewing

Tap List

ROBSON STREET HEFEWEIZEN

5% ABV

This was the first Hefeweizen to hit the patios in Vancouver and it's still one of the best ones in B.C.

BROCKTON IPA

6% ABV | 45 IBU

Released for GIB's twenty-fifth anniversary in 2009, this is a mid-level IPA—halfway between a timid English IPA and a hophead's dream.

IMPERIAL IPA (seasonal)

8.2% ABV | 100 IBU!

This is one of my favourite B.C. beers: the complex, citrus-pine hops are perfectly balanced by a solid malt base.

LIONS WINTER ALE (seasonal)

5.5% ABV

GIB's super-popular winter seasonal, this creamy, medium-dark ale has a slightly sweet caramel malt body with a big vanilla finish.

||||||||||||||||||||||||||||||||||||||||||||||

SHOCKWAVES RIPPLED THROUGH the craft beer community in B.C. back in 2009 when word came out that Granville Island Brewing had been purchased by Molson-Coors via its subsidiary, Creemore Springs. One of B.C.'s first micros dating back to 1984, the brewery grew from its small, original facility on Granville Island to become the city's favourite local brewer, with all of its beer styles named after popular city sites (English Bay Pale Ale, Kitsilano Maple Cream Ale, etc.) and its marketing focused on living the good life on the West Coast—"It's good to be here."

The brewery voluntarily left the B.C. Craft Brewer's Guild and beer geeks (me included) stopped buying GIB beer. But the truth of the matter was that Granville Island had been owned by a large commercial winery for a long time before that, with most of the beer actually being brewed at the winery's facility in Kelowna. When Molson took over, they shifted the main production of GIB's core brands to Vancouver's big Molson plant at the south end of the Burrard Street Bridge.

And, just as had happened with Creemore Springs, an Ontario craft brewery that Molson had bought back in 2005, nothing actually changed at Granville Island. If anything, the beer might have even improved a bit since the Molson plant offered state-of-the-art brewing equipment with a level of hygiene and consistency that might not have been achieved previously.

Most importantly to me, the original facility on Granville Island, which had long been used by brewmaster Vern Lambourne for making special seasonal beers, was not changed in any way—until it was renovated in 2012 to improve the brewhouse, tasting room and kitchen facilities. Lambourne is a skilled brewer, and his monthly rotation of seasonal beers includes some of the best beers brewed in B.C., including his Imperial IPA, Cascadian Dark Ale, Saison and Imperial Chocolate Stout.

Facts & Figures

OPENED › *1984* ✪ **STYLES PRODUCED** › *8 + many seasonals* ✪ **WHERE TO BUY** › *Everywhere in B.C.* ✪ **ON TAP** › *Everywhere in Vancouver, and many spots elsewhere in B.C.* ✪ **GROWLERS** › *No*

BREWERY CREEK

Vancouver's
earliest breweries

••••••••••••••••••••••••

WHEN MY WIFE and I first moved to Vancouver in 2001, we ended up renting an apartment one block west of Main Street at Fifteenth and Quebec. I remember I had a naïve impression that Main Street was a rough "East Van" area, but as I got to know the neighbourhood, I really fell in love with it. Some people were starting to call that area South Main or SoMa at the time. New restaurants started showing up there, followed by local fashion boutiques and, later, new condos. Eventually, this gentrification process forced us to seek less expensive housing elsewhere, but I have very fond memories of our time there.

When I was first exploring the area, I discovered a few plinths with historical plaques close to the intersection of Main Street and Kingsway that referred to the neighbourhood as "Brewery Creek." I was intrigued. It turns out that a stream once ran roughly along present-day Main Street from Tea Swamp (east of Main between Twelfth and Sixteenth Avenues) down to False Creek, which used to extend much farther east, all the way to where Clark Drive is now. This area, which early city planners called Mount Pleasant, became Vancouver's first suburb as the city began to grow beyond the downtown peninsula. And it also became the home of many of Vancouver's original breweries, including the City and Mainland

Breweries (both founded in 1887) and the Columbia Brewery (1888), which chose to build along the stream—giving it the name, Brewery Creek.

For the next twenty years (before it was covered over by streets and sewers), Brewery Creek provided the water for a succession of breweries, including the Alexander Brewery (Sixth Avenue and Scotia Street), Doering and Marstrand (Seventh Avenue and Scotia Street), the San Francisco Brewery (Eleventh Avenue and Main Street), and the Vancouver Brewery (Sixth Avenue and Scotia Street), a red-brick building built in 1903 which still stands today, now converted into artist live-work studios. There was even a giant waterwheel that powered the original Doering brewery.

Brewery Creek's time as the centre of the brewing industry in Vancouver was short-lived, no doubt partially because the creek itself disappeared along with many others that flowed down to False Creek. Today, however, there are some interesting connections to that history. One of the original buildings from the Vancouver Brewery complex, which was used for much of the twentieth century as an auto mechanic's shop, was renovated as part of a condo development in 2011, and the new Main Street Brewery plans to set up shop there in early 2013. Brassneck Brewery is setting up shop right around the corner on Main Street at Sixth Avenue. And farther "downstream" on First Avenue just off of Great Northern Way, Red Truck Brewing is building its new production brewery almost exactly where Brewery Creek once drained into False Creek.

There are a few other interesting historical connections in the neighbourhood, too. Brewery Creek Liquor Store (Fifteenth Avenue and Main Street) is one of the best places to buy craft beer in the city today, and a popular local restaurant, the Cascade Room (Tenth Avenue and Main Street), is named after Vancouver Brewery's flagship Cascade Beer, "The Beer Without Peer," as a 1907 advertisement claimed.

www.parallel49brewing.com
604-558-BREW (2739)
1950 Triumph Street, Vancouver
E-MAIL info@parallel49brewing.com
TWITTER @Parallel49beer

Parallel 49 Brewing

||||||||||||||||||||||||||||||||||||||||||||||

THIS BREWERY IS the baby of the business partners behind St. Augustine's, one of Vancouver's best taphouses that is second only to the Alibi Room in beer selection. Running that popular Commercial Drive eatery was ideal market research for Parallel 49, which hit the ground running hard when it opened in the spring of 2012 and hasn't looked back since.

To set up and run this brewery, Parallel 49's owners hired Graham With, a local star homebrewer with an engineering degree from UBC. They immediately flew to China with him to complete the purchase of their brewhouse equipment. With the boom in craft brewing across North America, it can take years to get new equipment from North American builders, and even with the distance and shipping costs, a brewhouse built in China costs far less than one built here.

The equipment arrived on With's thirtieth birthday, but unfortunately, the two Chinese engineers who were supposed to accompany it did not—they had not been granted visas by Canadian officials. After enlisting the aid of a local MP, the Parallel 49 partners finally got the help they needed and started brewing their first batches of beer on Easter weekend, 2012.

Tap List

HOPARAZZI

6% ABV | 50 IBU

This India Pale Lager is pale gold and refreshingly crisp with a subtle bite of citrusy West Coast hops.

OLD BOY

5% ABV | 25 IBU

A tribute to English pub beers, this is a well-balanced brown ale.

GYPSY
TEARS RUBY ALE

6% ABV | 40 IBU

A ruby red ale with a solid malt base that showcases some aromatic West Coast hops.

SEEDSPITTER (seasonal)

5% ABV | 8 IBU

A summer wit beer with a watermelon twist. Light, refreshing and delicious.

This big brewery was built from scratch and designed to pump out a lot of beer, so Parallel 49 is obviously planning to be a major player in the market. They've adopted a fun, cartoony branding style, and so far, at least, they've chosen beer styles that are a mix of old school fundamentals—such as Old Boy, a brown ale—and cutting-edge experimentation. One of their core brands is an India Pale Lager, and their first summer seasonal was a watermelon wit, which is unique in B.C. Initially, there was no hoppy IPA in sight even though that is the flagship style for most West Coast craft breweries, but With said he was waiting to get the right hops before he finally released the cheekily named Lord of the Hops early in 2013.

Parallel 49 has bombarded the market with excellent limited releases in 650 mL bombers over its first year in business, including: Lost Souls Chocolate Pumpkin Porter, Salty Scot (a sea-salted caramel scotch ale), Black Christmas CDA, Vow of Silence (a Belgian Trappist-style quadrupel), and a Russian Imperial Stout.

....
Facts & Figures

OPENED ▸ *2012* ✪ **STYLES PRODUCED** ▸ *7 + seasonals* ✪ **WHERE TO BUY** ▸ *At the brewery and in liquor stores throughout B.C.* ✪ **ON TAP** ▸ *Throughout Vancouver* ✪ **GROWLERS** ▸ *Yes*

www.powellbeer.com
604-558-2537
1830 Powell Street, Vancouver
TWITTER @PowellBeer

Powell Street Craft Brewery

||||||||||||||||||||||||||||||||||||||||

IN JULY 2011, David Bowkett decided to turn his love of craft beer into more than just a home brewing hobby. The Powell Street Craft Brewery opened a year and a half later. Bowkett and his wife, Nicole, created an inviting storefront atmosphere where traditional half-gallon growlers and one-litre versions they call "Boston Rounds" can be bought and filled, along with pre-filled 650 mL bottles. Powell Street is focusing on three core brands—a pale ale, porter and hoppy IPA—but Bowkett says he intends to experiment from time to time with one-off brews of other interesting styles.

Bowkett still works at his day job as an architectural technologist, brewing on evenings and weekends, but he did give up his career as vocalist for a hardcore punk band called Third Lit to start the brewery. Be sure to sneak a peek at his tattooed arms while he is filling your growler.

Tap List

DIVE BOMB PORTER

5% ABV | 33 IBU

Named for the iconic East Vancouver crows who are known to attack unwary pedestrians, this porter is rich and malty with a great roasted character.

OLD JALOPY PALE ALE

5.5% ABV | 40 IBU

An English-style pale ale with some peppy Northwest hops. Winner of Beer of the Year at the 2013 Canadian Brewing Awards.

Facts & Figures

OPENED › *2012* ✪ **STYLES PRODUCED ›** *3 + seasonals*
✪ **WHERE TO BUY ›** *At the brewery or at private liquor stores in Vancouver* ✪ **ON TAP ›** *Several taphouses and restaurants in Vancouver.* ✪ **GROWLERS ›** *Yes*

TAPPING THE CASK

Vancouver's
Cask Beer Scene

••••••••••••••••••••••

CASK-CONDITIONED BEER undergoes a secondary fermentation in a sealed vessel, often with special added ingredients such as hops or other flavouring agents, and then is served directly from the cask without being filtered or pasteurized. The yeast remains with the beer, gently carbonating and conditioning it. The beer is essentially "alive" right up until the moment you drink it.

The cask typically used is a metal barrel known as a firkin, which holds approximately forty litres or eighty pints. This is a size that allows it to be transported relatively easily. It is also reasonably possible to empty a firkin in just a few hours so pubs will often just prop the cask on top of a bar until it is empty. Bars that have regular casks on tap use a refrigeration system to keep the beer at a proper "cellar temperature" no matter when it is served.

Known as "real ale" in the UK, cask beer was long the traditional method of brewing in Britain, but as bigger breweries took over the market there, it began to disappear in favour of mass-market bottled beers. This led to the formation of the Campaign For Real Ale (CAMRA) in 1971, which has helped revitalize the brewing of traditional ales in the UK and around the world.

Cask conditioning allows the malt and hop flavours to deepen and expand so the resulting beer is usually richer and more complex than typical beer from a keg or bottle. Brewers love to experiment by either adding something special to the cask or by testing a new recipe they've never tried before. Either way, it's a chance to taste a unique and delicious brew you can't get anywhere else.

Dix BBQ & Brewery was the first place in Vancouver to hold a regular monthly cask event starting in July 2002. A year later, they began tapping casks weekly on Thursday evenings. But Barry Benson, the B in R&B Brewing, says that there were a few one-offs in the years before that. He remembers tapping a cask of their Auld Nick Winter Ale in 1998 at the old Fogg n' Suds restaurant on West Broadway, an early haven for beer lovers in Vancouver.

In late 2006, R&B Brewing put together a weekly event at The Whip restaurant called Real Ale Sundays. R&B played a major role in organizing the event for the first three years or so, talking to other brewers, encouraging them to supply casks, and filling in with their own casks when needed. Eventually, as cask events began catching on in other restaurants, more and more breweries got on board and started producing casks of their own. But R&B is still the premier cask brewery in Vancouver with ninety firkins and ten pins (half-size casks) in their inventory.

There are now casks tapped every night somewhere in Vancouver, and places like the Cascade Room, Irish Heather and Alibi Room keep casks on all the time. CAMRA Vancouver hosts a major cask event with each new season and Central City Brewing hosts a very popular cask festival each summer and winter at its brewpub in Surrey.

Here is a list of places that host regular cask nights in the city:

The Whip (209 East Sixth Avenue)
Real Ale Sundays—Sundays at 4:00 PM

St. Augustine's (2360 Commercial Drive)
Cask Mondays—Mondays at 6:00 PM

Railway Club (579 Dunsmuir Street)
Rail Ale Tuesdays—Tuesdays at 5:00 PM

Yaletown Brewing Company (1111 Mainland Street)
Making It Real (Ale)—Thursdays at 4:00 PM

London Pub (700 Main Street)
Tap That Cask—Fridays at 5:00 PM

Alibi Room (157 Alexander Street)
Three casks on tap all the time

Cascade Room (2616 Main Street)
R&B cask on tap all the time

Irish Heather (210 Carrall Street)
R&B's Red Devil Pale Ale on cask all the time

www.r-and-b.com
604-874-ALES (2537)
54 East Fourth Avenue, Vancouver
E-MAIL ales@r-and-b.com
TWITTER @RandBBrewing

R&B Brewing

|||||||||||||||||||||||||||||||||||||||||||||||||

RICK DELLOW AND BARRY BENSON, the *R* and *B* in R&B Brewing, became friends while working at the Vancouver Molson plant in the 1980s. A little later, they worked together at Newlands, an Abbotsford-based company that makes brewing equipment. After several years installing new brewhouses at places like Steamworks, Russell and Granville Island, as well as elsewhere around the world, Benson and Dellow decided they wanted to start their own brewery.

R&B Brewing is proud of its independent spirit—the founders say they wanted the brewery to "stand in opposition to what the beer world had become—big, non-descript, faceless and corporate." Back in 1997, the Main Street neighbourhood where they opened was definitely East Van edgy, even if the official dividing line between east and west in the city is Ontario Street, only half a block away. An address in that area is now much more desirable than it would have been fifteen years ago, when I'm sure they picked it for an attractive price tag. The snazzy new Olympic Village is practically across the street from them.

As the neighbourhood has grown and evolved, so too has R&B Brewing. Now, the

Tap List

SUN GOD WHEAT ALE
4.2% ABV | 12 IBU
A light, flavourful wheat beer ideal for summer patio sipping.

RED DEVIL PALE ALE
5.2% ABV | 28 IBU
A rich, reddish pale ale with a floral hop aroma and malty sweetness.

RAVEN CREAM ALE
4.8% ABV | 18 IBU
A "Vancouver cream ale" (a la Shaftebury and Russell) that is unexpectedly dark for the style, this is a tasty beer with a nutty, roasted character.

HOPPELGANGER IPA
6% ABV | 45 IBU
Not the hoppiest of IPAs, this is a good introductory beer for wannabe hopheads.

plucky company employs ten people and has expanded into the neighbouring building. One of the reasons for its successful growth is R&B's specialization in cask-conditioned beer. As the cask beer movement took hold in Vancouver about ten years ago at places like The Whip restaurant, just a few blocks away, R&B recognized this niche market and became the go-to brewery for casks. Now, with cask nights every night of the week somewhere in the city, and casks on full-time at the Alibi Room, the Irish Heather and elsewhere, you'll find many of them are R&B's.

Until recently, R&B only released their beer on tap and in 650 mL bombers, but in fall 2012 they started canning some of their beers, which should open them up to even bigger markets.

Facts & Figures

OPENED ‣ *1997* ✪ **STYLES PRODUCED** ‣ *8 + seasonals* ✪ **WHERE TO BUY** ‣ *Liquor stores in Vancouver area and on Vancouver Island* ✪ **ON TAP** ‣ *Throughout Vancouver* ✪ **GROWLERS** ‣ *Yes*

www.redtruckbeer.com
604-682-4733
315 First Avenue East, Vancouver
E-MAIL info@redtruckbeer.com
TWITTER @redtruckbeer

Red Truck Beer

Tap List

RED TRUCK ALE
5.1% ABV
A solid, dependable ale.
Nothing special, but very
drinkable.

RED TRUCK LAGER
4.9% ABV
A solid, dependable lager. If
this sounds repetitive, you
get the picture.

||||||||||||||||||||||||||||||||||||||||||||||

STARTED AS A draft-only brand by the Mark
James Group, which runs a chain of brewpubs in Vancouver, Surrey and Whistler, Red
Truck Beer has been brewed at the North
Vancouver brewpub, Taylor's Crossing, even
after it was closed. Mark James is now building a new truck stop–themed production
brewery on First Avenue just off of Great
Northern Way, to open in the fall of 2013.
The brewery will also produce beers under
the Yaletown Brewing banner.

Dave Varga has been "Da Brewa" responsible for Red Truck Beer from the get-go, and
he is highly respected in Vancouver beer circles, especially for his specialty brews, which
often appear at cask festivals and other beer
events in the region. It will be interesting to
see what he comes up with as he is able to
flex his muscles in the new facility.

Facts & Figures

OPENED ▸ *2005* ✪ **STYLES PRODUCED** ▸ *2 + seasonals* ✪
ON TAP ▸ *Throughout Greater Vancouver* ✪ **GROWLERS** ▸ *No*

VANCOUVER
CRAFT BEER WEEK

....

Held for nine days at the end of May each year

SINCE ITS launch in 2010, Vancouver Craft Beer Week has grown into one of the biggest events in B.C.'s festival calendar. With signature and satellite events put on by the VCBW organizers and affiliated events put on by individual breweries, pubs and restaurants, it is estimated that more than 25,000 people attended VCBW events in 2012.

Some of the most popular events each year include the quick-to-sell-out Hoppapalooza, hosted by Nigel Springthorpe at the Alibi Room; the Cicerone vs. Sommelier beer- and wine-pairing contest; Sisters of the Tap (previously Women in Beer); and the two-night VCBW Beer Festival that closes out the week. Personally, I am a big fan of the Belgian Showcase held at the two Biercraft locations.

The major events go on sale in advance through the VCBW website, but many of the associated events are not ticketed so there are always plenty of opportunities to join in the fun.

www.vancouvercraftbeerweek.com

www.steamworks.com
604-689-2739
375 Water Street, Vancouver
E-MAIL info@steamworks.com

Steamworks Brew Pub

Tap List

PILSNER

5.2% ABV | 35 IBU
Winner of Beer of the Year at the 2011 and 2012 B.C. Beer Awards, this pitch-perfect Pilsner is full-bodied and surprisingly hoppy.

WHEAT ALE

5% ABV | 8 IBU
Known as Ipanema for years, this classic Belgian white ale is flavoured with coriander and Curacoa orange peel.

HEROICA
OATMEAL STOUT

5% ABV | 30 IBU
Thick and chocolaty with a dry finish. A great stout.

FRAMBOZEN (seasonal)

7% ABV | 16 IBU
Famous for the "Frambozen accidents" this used to cause when it was a surprisingly quaffable 9% ABV, this raspberry ale has been toned down a bit for the bottle.

||||||||||||||||||||||||||||||||||||||||||||||

THE REAL ESTATE mantra of "location, location, location" could certainly be applied to Steamworks, which occupies one of the best spots in downtown Vancouver—right next to Waterfront Station at the edge of Gastown, the city's oldest neighbourhood which is now one of its most tourist-friendly areas. Anyone could be successful there, and one might expect to find a big chain restaurant or a pseudo-brewpub with basic, boring beer there, but instead, Vancouverites and visitors to the city have been blessed with a top-notch brewpub that has been serving up excellent, interesting beers and great food since 1995.

My first visit to Steamworks was as a brewers' groupie (a brewpie?). My friend Ken, the first brewer at Kelowna's Tree Brewing in the mid-'90s, was serving beer at the Autumn Brewmasters' festival at the Plaza of Nations in Vancouver so I followed him around the event all day. The real highlight was when I got to tag along to the after-festival brewers' party at Steamworks.

The brewpub had just opened, and to my eye (and taste buds), it was incredible. The cellar where the brewhouse is situated seemed ancient already, like something you'd find in a centuries-old pub in London, and I've never grown tired of that room in all the intervening years. We were given a "backstage tour" of the operation where we were shown the steam pipe that is used to heat the brew kettle—the same steam line that powers the nearby clock that draws tourists to Gastown for its steam whistle chimes every quarter hour. The original name for the brewpub was actually Quarterdeck, but when they discovered the steam pipe running through their building and realized they could use it in the brewing process, the new name and concept were born.

Since then, Steamworks has consistently brewed great beer in its magnificent setting, never sacrificing quality to increase profits or to cater to the ravening hordes, even while increasing seats in its various dining rooms from the original 60 up to its current 750 or so—making it, according to owner Eli Gershkovitch, "the biggest non-Chinese restaurant in Vancouver." Gershkovitch says he fell in love with the brewpub concept while travelling in Belgium and wanted to replicate it here when he came home.

In 2012, Steamworks underwent a rebranding of its marketing image to launch a new line of bottled products, adopting a playful, illustrated "steampunk lite" style. As the brewhouse has been working at capacity for years just to supply the brewpub, the bottled beer will be brewed on contract by Dead Frog Brewery until Steamworks can open a separate brewing facility, which they hope will be completed by late 2013.

Facts & Figures

OPENED ‣ *1995* ⚙ **STYLES PRODUCED** ‣ *6 + seasonals* ⚙
WHERE TO BUY ‣ *Liquor stores throughout the province* ⚙
ON TAP ‣ *The brewpub* ⚙ **GROWLERS** ‣ *Yes*

www.stormbrewing.org
604-255-9119
310 Commercial Drive, Vancouver
E-MAIL james@stormbrewing.org
TWITTER @StormBrewingVan

Storm Brewing

||||||||||||||||||||||||||||||||||||||||||||||||||

"WELCOME TO MY underground lair," says James Walton, his sinister greeting defeated by the huge grin on his face. The ramshackle brewery at the gritty northern end of Commercial Drive is not exactly a shining example of cleanliness, but there's no doubting the quality of the beer that Walton has produced here for nearly twenty years.

Walton uses "Super Genius" as his e-mail tag line, but "Mad Scientist" would fit just as well. He looks and dresses like a punk rock star, and jokes that he got into the brewing business "for the fame aspect."

Originally from Port Alberni, he studied at UBC, then tried running an exotic mushroom farm before deciding to open a brewery in 1994. He cobbled together equipment from scrapyards and began brewing in the roughest of circumstances. His first beer, Red Sky Alt, was a big hit in Vancouver, and he also brewed a porter for a time. He considered brewing an IPA back then, but says Tall Ship (a Squamish brewery that existed for a few years in the mid-1990s) was doing one well and he didn't want to step on their toes. After they went under, he "waited a suitable mourning period," and then introduced Hurricane IPA, which he still brews today.

Tap List

BLACK PLAGUE STOUT

8.5% ABV

Once a winter seasonal, Storm now brews this black behemoth year-round.

HIGHLAND SCOTTISH ALE

5% ABV

Vancouver beer writer and Scottish émigré Jan Zeschky says this is as close to the real thing as it gets. Creamy, nutty, malty and delicious.

HURRICANE IPA

7% ABV

Vancouver's original IPA and still going strong. Often available on cask with some extra goodie in the mix.

IMPERIAL FLANDERS RED ALE

11% ABV

This beer is surprising quaffable for its alcohol potency and wild yeast sourness.

Walton says that original "cloudy, bitter ale" was not well received, partially because he dry-hopped every keg, which sometimes left chunks of hops floating in pint glasses—"scary for the uninitiated." He remembers how the co-manager of the Railway Club, Steve Forsyth, balked at the sight, saying he couldn't sell it. It turns out that Forsyth now runs the Eagle Ridge organic hop farm in Mission, which he started in part to support local brewers during the hops shortage several years ago.

Eventually, Walton swapped out the Red Sky Alt for Highland Scottish Ale, replaced the porter with the Black Plague Stout, and added an authentic Czech Pilsner, which are all still brewed. Each beer is an ideal example of its style. Storm's other specialty is sour beers, an experiment Walton began in 1997 after Yaletown Brewing brewmaster Iain Hill encouraged him to re-pitch some yeast cultures from leftover spoiled beer in old kegs. The last of this sour lambic, aged for twelve years in oak casks, was released in 2010 and won accolades.

Still on the sour side, Walton is now focusing on the Flanders red ale style, which is not quite as mouth-puckeringly sour as a lambic. Aged at least a year in the same oak casks, the result is a potent reddish-hued beer with a sourness that is refreshing and satisfying—and surprisingly drinkable for a beer with 11 per cent ABV.

Walton is well known for adding pretty much anything to a cask of beer just to see what the result will taste like. For example: Basil IPA brewed for Italian Days on the Drive (delicious, and made me crave pizza); and Echinacea Stout (much less successful although good for my immune system, presumably).

When I visited the quintessential East Vancouver brewery, I just missed tasting a special fresh-hopped cask he "grew, picked, brewed, casked, delivered and drank" himself. It was called 100% James. Maybe he is in it for the fame after all.

....

Facts & Figures

OPENED ‣ *1994* ◉ **STYLES PRODUCED** ‣ *5 + seasonals for every crazy idea James has* ◉ **ON TAP** ‣ *Throughout Greater Vancouver* ◉ **GROWLERS** ‣ *No*

NIGEL'S ALIBI

In Search of Craft Beer

....

I ARRIVE JUST at opening time and claim a stool at the bar. The twenty-foot-long row of taps, up to fifty now, is both awe-inspiring and intimidating. What to try tonight? I check the chalkboard to see what casks are on and pick a dry-hopped Swans Extra IPA to sip while I scan the typewritten tap list, smartly divided by style: lagers, wheats, IPAS, sours and Belgians. Ah, the Alibi Room. There's nowhere else like it.

On top of the incredible beer selection, it's in a great building: a century-old heritage brick structure right next to the train tracks—you can watch the West Coast Express go by right outside the windows behind the bar. It has wonderful old hardwood floors, solid beams and tall windows.

Behind the bar is Nigel Springthorpe, who went from employee to co-owner and manager back in 2006. At that time, he was just starting to get interested in craft beer, and over the next few years he systematically sought out new and interesting beer wherever he could find it, first from B.C. craft brewers, then later from farther south down the Cascadian coast, and finally from European sources.

"It was never really the plan," he admits in his characteristic British accent, "but as my own tastes changed and I started to discover the wonderful world of craft beer, I decided to explore the possibility of putting all of the best breweries, near and far, side by side in one location."

As the Alibi Room's row of taps grew to a dozen, then two dozen, then up to the current fifty plus three cask engines, the city's beer lovers arrived in droves and brewers clamoured to get their beers served there. A healthy sense of competition among the beer makers pushed them to create better and better beer, to be accepted by both Nigel's increasingly discerning palate and the ever-growing ranks of craft beer lovers seeking new and more challenging styles.

Other craft beer-focused places have followed the Alibi Room's lead in Vancouver, including St. Augustine's on Commercial Drive, the two Biercraft locations, Rogue's two outlets and Portland Craft, among others, but none quite have the vibe that Nigel created in Gastown. And now, in one of those full-circle stories that writers love, he hopes to make a new mark on the scene with the launch of the Brassneck Brewery in 2013.

Alibi Room
157 Alexander Street (@ Main)
604-623-3383
www.alibi.ca

www.markjamesgroup.com/
yaletown.html
604-681-2739
1111 Mainland Street, Vancouver
E-MAIL ybc@mjg.ca

Yaletown Brewing Company

||||||||||||||||||||||||||||||||||||||||||||||

DATING BACK TO 1994, Yaletown Brewing is the oldest brewpub in Vancouver, although you wouldn't know it by looking at it since it fits right in among the high-class shops and restaurants lining Yaletown's trendy streets. YBC was actually part of the movement that transformed the Yaletown neighbourhood from an older, rundown warehouse district into the popular area it is today. And with the addition of the nearby Yaletown station of the Canada Line in time for the 2010 Winter Olympics, the brewpub's incredible location is better than ever.

YBC is the flagship in the Mark James Group chain, which once featured four excellent brewpubs in the greater Vancouver area. Despite being extremely popular in the craft beer scene, Dix BBQ & Brewery was closed in 2010, and Taylor's Crossing was also shuttered early in 2012, although the brewing facility is still being used to brew the Red Truck brand until their new production brewery is finished in the fall of 2013. Mark James also operates the BrewHouse in Whistler village. (See "Why Are There So Few Brewpubs in Vancouver?" on page 91.)

The large building has a smaller pub on the west end with pool tables, TVs and a

Tap List

BRICK & BEAM IPA
5.8% ABV | 65 IBU
Won B.C. Beer of the Year in 2010. I stop by whenever I'm in the neighbourhood so I can enjoy this excellent IPA.

HILL'S SPECIAL WHEAT
5% ABV
An excellent and very authentic Hefeweizen.

LE NEZ ROUGE (seasonal)
9% ABV
A Belgian Tripel that will definitely turn your nose red.

OUD BRUIN (seasonal)
5% ABV
Hill's pièce de résistance, this is a complex and challenging sour beer, aged for a year in oak barrels and brewed with several yeast and bacterial cultures.

small patio overlooking the street. There is a larger full-service restaurant on the other side with a spacious patio ideal for people-watching spread around the entire corner block. In terms of seeing and being seen, Yaletown is one of Vancouver's primary GLBT-friendly neighbourhoods, so it's quite possible to catch the eye of attractive people of both sexes on any given night.

Brewmaster Iain Hill has been at the helm of Yaletown Brewing (and the chain as a whole) since the start, and he is widely respected as one of the leaders of the city's craft beer community. His beers are excellent across the board. When Dix closed, Hill brought its famous cask night to YBC: every Thursday at 4:00 PM, he taps a creative, cask-conditioned version of one his standard brews. (See page 101 for more on cask events in Vancouver.)

The only negative about YBC is that despite it being a brewpub, the beer can become a little lost among cocktail events, stag and/or doe parties, DJ'd music events, and so on. But if that's the price of keeping Iain's excellent beer on tap in such a prime location, I'll take it any time—as long as they keep the deep-fried pickles on the menu.

Facts & Figures

OPENED ▸ *1994* ✪ **STYLES PRODUCED** ▸ *6 + seasonals* ✪
WHERE TO BUY ▸ *In growlers at the brewpub* ✪ **ON TAP** ▸
The brewpub ✪ **GROWLERS** ▸ *Yes*

TAPHOUSES

Vancouver

••••••••••••••••••••••••

VANCOUVER IS blessed with several excellent taphouses that serve a wide variety of craft beer from B.C. and elsewhere. Here are my top five.

Alibi Room
157 Alexander Street
First not just alphabetically, this is B.C.'s Craft Beer HQ with fifty taps and three casks. If you are only in Vancouver for one night, go to the Alibi—but get there early or be prepared to wait in line.

Biercraft Bistro (Two locations)
3305 Cambie Street
1191 Commercial Drive
Incredible Belgian-focused beer list, with knowledgeable staff and glassware to match every beer.

Portland Craft
3835 Main Street
The best place to drink beer in SoMa, the focus here is on craft beer from Portland.

St. Augustine's
2360 Commercial Drive
Second only to the Alibi Room in terms of beer selections, this is where I go to watch the Canucks and drink craft beer.

Tap & Barrel
1 Athletes Way
This Olympic Village venue has a great tap list and an incredible two-level patio overlooking False Creek.

BOTTLE SHOPS
Vancouver

....

VANCOUVER HAS several excellent private liquor stores that feature extensive craft beer collections. Here is the crème de la crème.

Brewery Creek
3045 Main Street

Cedar Cottage
3728 Clark Drive
(at Kingsway)

Crosstown Liquor Store
568 Abbott Street

Darby's
2001 MacDonald Street

Firefly
2857 Cambie Street

Hastings Liquor
2769 East Hastings Street

Legacy
1633 Manitoba Street
(Olympic Village)

Libations
928 West King Edward
Avenue

Steamworks Beer and Wine Shop
375 Water Street

Viti
900 Seymour Street

West Coast Liquor
(Two locations)
6295 Fraser Street
5503 West Boulevard

BEST BEERS

Vancouver

●●●●●●●●●●●●●●●●●●●●●●●

Coal Harbour Triumph Rye Ale
I love rye ales for their nutty, earthy, dry malt flavour: this is the only one regularly brewed in B.C.

Granville Island Brewing Imperial IPA
I buy a lot of this beer when it is out early each year: it's the perfect winter warmer with an incredible kaleidoscope of hop flavours.

Parallel 49 Brewing Hay Fever Saison
The first time I tasted this spicy, slightly sour, and oh-so-refreshing farmhouse ale, I immediately thought of Dupont's Saison, the benchmark for the style.

Steamworks Pilsner
Pilsners don't get much better than this winner of the Best Beer in B.C. two years running (2011 and 2012).

Yaletown Brewing Brick & Beam IPA
Since I moved to Victoria, my visits to the brewpub have become few and far between, so I can't wait for Yaletown to begin bottling this excellent IPA.

RICHMOND, SURREY & FRASER VALLEY

AT THE BREWERY	DRAFT	FOOD	GROWLERS	BOTTLE SALES	TOURS	BEDS
Big Ridge Brewing	✪	✪	✪		✪	
Big River Brewpub	✪	✪		✪	✪	
Central City Brewing	✪	✪	✪	✪	✪	
Dead Frog Brewery				✪	✪	
Mission Springs Brewpub	✪	✪	✪	✪	✪	
Old Yale Brewing					✪	
Russell Brewing				✪	✪	

SIPPING
IN THE SUBURBS

....

IF YOU LIVE in the Greater Vancouver area, you know that Vancouver's suburbs often get a bad rap as soulless commuter communities with no character of their own. Not so, particularly when it comes to what's important: good beer. Craft beer is well established here, with four breweries and three brewpubs spread from Richmond all the way out to Chilliwack, and more on the way. Some of these breweries and brewpubs are where they are because it is far cheaper to set up and run a business there than it is in Vancouver. But some are there because that's where they want to be: serving the local community's interest in craft beer. And there's history here, too. Hops were once a major agricultural crop in B.C., and the Fraser Valley was the epicentre of that industry, Chilliwack in particular. Hundreds, perhaps even thousands of migrant workers would help harvest the crop each fall, many of them travelling up the coast picking hops in Oregon and Washington before joining the crowd here (see "Brewer's Gold" on page 140).

One of the suburbs in this group, Surrey, is poised to catch up with and perhaps even surpass Vancouver itself in terms of population over the next twenty-five years. At present, there are only two brewpubs and one brewery in Surrey, but that doesn't describe the full picture. Central City, a brewpub in the heart of Surrey's "new downtown" area, is building a huge new production facility near the Patullo Bridge which will make it a major player in the province's beer scene—it already is in terms of the quality of its products, but it just doesn't have enough capacity at the brewpub to fill demand for its beer.

The current wave of expansion in B.C.'s craft beer industry seems to be mainly focused on Vancouver—after years of relative dormancy, the province's largest city has finally fallen in love with craft beer. But I predict another wave will follow in the suburban communities around the city: new brewpubs and breweries that will meet demand from local beer lovers who have joined the craft beer revolution and want to enjoy it right in their own neighbourhoods. Indeed, new operations are already planned for New Westminster, Delta and Richmond.

www.markjamesgroup.com/
bigridge.html
604-574-2739
5580 152nd Street, Surrey
E-MAIL bigridge@mjg.ca

Big Ridge Brewing Co.

||||||||||||||||||||||||||||||||||||||||||||

PART OF THE Mark James Group chain that once included five brewpubs in total, but now is down to three, Big Ridge is their outpost in Surrey. Unfortunately, it is not close to the SkyTrain so you need a car or a whole lot of patience with bus connections to visit if you're coming from Vancouver. Too bad it's hard to get to because it's a great brewpub with a relaxed, comfortable atmosphere and a top-notch brewer at the helm in Tariq Khan.

Khan, a Montrealer by birth, took over from the previous brewer, Tony Dewalt, a legend in B.C. brewing circles who earned his reputation at Dix before Mark James closed down that popular brewpub. Khan learned his craft in the UK, including a stint at the Dark Star Brewery in West Sussex just south of London, which specializes in cask-conditioned beers.

Khan is somewhat limited in the styles of beer he can brew by the neighbourhood's traditional palate—his Harvest Lager is definitely the pub's biggest seller. Even the more challenging beers are given safe names to keep them from deterring customers who are not familiar with them. For instance, his Hefeweizen is just a "wheat beer" (though it's

Tap List

CHIMNEY HILL WHEAT

4.5% ABV | 12 IBU

An excellent and very authentic Hefeweizen even if the name doesn't say so.

CLOVER ALE

6.3% ABV | 65 IBU

Again, you wouldn't know it from the name, but this is a well-made IPA—with no clover anywhere near it.

AMARILLO ALE (seasonal)

5.5% ABV | 35 IBU

A delicious session IPA that highlights the fruity, Tang-like flavour profile of Amarillo hops.

WRATH OF KHAN BELGIAN IPA (seasonal)

6.9% ABV | 75 IBU

Brewmaster Tariq Khan is famous for this crossover beer. Spicy, hoppy, delicious!

actually a great Hef), and the IPA is called Clover Ale, a twist on the nearby Cloverdale area.

It's too bad Khan doesn't have free rein because whenever he does try something different, it's usually exceptional. He is well known in the Vancouver beer scene, ironically, because Nigel Springthorpe has been a champion of his from early on, putting his special beers on tap at the Alibi Room whenever Khan brews one. That said, Khan regularly tries out new specialty beers on the local crowd whenever he gets the opportunity and enough space in the fermentation tanks. He taps a special cask-conditioned beer at the bar every Friday, and the Surrey Beer Club holds regular events at the brewpub, for which he tries to make a special cask or two.

Facts & Figures

OPENED ‣ *1999 (moved across the street in 2010)* ✪ **STYLES PRODUCED** ‣ *5 + seasonals* ✪ **WHERE TO BUY** ‣ *At the brewpub* ✪ **ON TAP** ‣ *The brewpub* ✪ **GROWLERS** ‣ *Yes*

RICHMOND
PUB CRAWL

....

RICHMOND, JUST SOUTH of Vancouver, has only one brewpub, Big River Brewpub, but it also has several restaurants and taphouses that feature craft beer. Easily accessible from Vancouver by transit using the Canada Line and connecting buses, there are several good options for a Richmond pub crawl. Some pubs even offer shuttles connecting with the Canada Line.

Fogg n' Sudds
10720 Cambie Road
604-273-0776

O'Hares Gastropub
5031 Steveston Highway
604-277-2305

Pumphouse Pub
6031 Blundell Road
604-274-7424

Steveston Village, down in the southwest corner of Richmond, is a historic fishing village known for the Gulf of Georgia Cannery, a National Historic Site. It's also home to a great little craft beer scene with three very different local restaurants offering diverse craft beer selections along with excellent food options. Personally, I think Steveston is a prime spot for a brewpub of its own—I know that would make my buddy John very happy!

Blue Canoe Waterfront Restaurant
140-3866 Bayview Street
604-275-7811

Gudrun
3500 Moncton Street
604-272-1991

Hog Shack
160-3900 Bayview Street
604-272-7264

Big River Brewpub

Tap List

RIVER PILOT ESB

5% ABV | 40 IBU

A solid ESB with a creamy, malty body underscored with a pleasant hop bitterness.

**INDIA
PALE ALE** (seasonal)

6.3% ABV | 60 IBU

Brewed in the British IPA tradition: it's definitely bitter but the hops are one-dimensional without much aroma or depth.

||||||||||||||||||||||||||||||||||||||||||||||||||

OK, TRIVIA TIME, kids: what are the two B.C. brewpubs attached to bowling alleys? (Start whistling the *Jeopardy!* theme song now.) Give up? The answer is: Big River in Richmond and Freddy's in Kelowna. And now for bonus points: how many B.C. breweries has Big River's current brewmaster, Michael Stewart, worked at over his long career in the industry? Four: Shaftebury, Legends (since closed), Backwoods (now Dead Frog) and Big River.

Stewart, whose grandfather was a brewer in England, got his start brewing beer at home for his dad and friends. After putting himself through a computer science program at college on the avails of his home brewing (no comment on the legality of such an enterprise), he got into the brewing business full time.

The beer at Big River is fairly good—better than the other bowling alley brewpub's lineup for sure—but it's not going to excite you much if you are a hop-lovin' beer geek. But if you like to sip a craft beer while you bowl, you could do worse than the ESB or stout.

Facts & Figures

OPENED ▸ *1997* ✱ **STYLES PRODUCED ▸** *7 + seasonals*
✱ **ON TAP ▸** *The brewpub* ✱ **GROWLERS ▸** *No*

A PASSION
FOR BREWING

Central City's Gary Lohin

·······················

CENTRAL CITY BREWING'S Gary Lohin is one of the leaders of
B.C.'s craft beer revolution. He is an undisputed master of the
brewing arts who always has time for a chat with a beer lover—
especially if it's about Red Racer Beer, Central City's flagship
line. Lohin also believes the craft beer community should work
together to grow as an industry, and does his part by hosting
cask events that feature other craft brewers at his brewpub
in Surrey.

Lohin got his start brewing at home back in his twenties
before entering the brewing industry as a Vancouver-area sales
rep for Whistler Brewing in the late 1980s. He got involved on
the brewing side near the end of his time there and then found
work as a brewer with Okanagan Spring Brewery in Vernon in
the early '90s, back in that brewery's heyday when they were
still brewing some excellent beers.

However, Lohin really made a name for himself as brewmaster for Sailor Hagar's brewpub in his own hometown of
North Vancouver. After several years there, the pub's management decided to stop brewing their own beer, but Lohin was
ready to run his own place, so he and two partners opened the
Central City brewpub in Surrey, Vancouver's largest suburb, in
2003. Central City took some risks to get noticed in those early

days, and back in 2007 and 2008 when Red Racer beers began showing up on liquor store shelves, the idea of craft beer *in cans* was pretty revolutionary.

But it was what was in those cans that mattered, and that excellent beer got the attention of B.C.'s beer lovers, especially those in Vancouver. Since then, Red Racer beer has been flying off the shelves and Lohin has been unable to keep up with demand, turning down requests from big restaurant chains, distributors south of the border and provincial liquor boards elsewhere in Canada. He manages to ship a pallet or two of Red Racer IPA to Ontario each summer—the LCBO sells those cans as singles for nearly double the cost here in B.C., and they still sell out in a matter of days.

Lohin is proud of his accomplishments, but not arrogant. He takes his craft seriously and doesn't believe in standing on his laurels. Does Central City's success challenge Vancouver's other brewers to step up? Maybe. Lohin says there is a good camaraderie among the city's brewers, but with a dash of healthy competition. "Everybody is pushing each other to make good beer. I think it's a good thing. It's healthy. But I do my own thing. I'm not influenced by anybody."

These days, what excites him most is Central City's coming expansion: a new brewing facility that will significantly increase capacity, add storage space for barrel aging and bottle conditioning, and allow him to bottle his specialty brews. The new brewery should be operational some time in 2013, and based on the excitement on his face, he can't wait.

"We just want this to go back to being a brewpub," Lohin says of the original facility. "No packaging. Go back to brewing and moving beer through the serving tanks. It could really be an R&D brewery for us, which would be great."

The new facility will be based on a 50-hL brew kettle, and with several 50-hL fermenting tanks available, he sees great potential. "It will make us more flexible," he explains. "I love the idea of making one style to see if it works—make a single batch and put it out in bombers and let it go and see what happens. Maybe I'll make three different IPAs with three different kinds of hops and see which one you like. Maybe I'll have a Cascadian Dark Ale out all the time, and have the Imperial IPA available as much as I can." With the local craft beer crowd's insatiable appetite, especially for Central City's beer, he would have little trouble selling all of it.

Lohin is also interested in distilling. "That's a wave I want to catch, not follow," he says. "We are designing a spot in the new brewery to put stills in. It might not happen right away, but we're going to have a spot for them."

Being named Canadian Brewer of the Year was a great honour. "Gotta give it to the boys in the brewery here," Lohin says, modestly redirecting the praise. "I try to hire people with passion. Once you do that, you have a solid backbone and it's hard to go wrong."

And that passion for brewing great craft beer starts with him.

www.centralcitybrewing.com
604-582-6620
13450-102nd Avenue, Surrey
E-MAIL info@centralcitybrewing.com
TWITTER @CentralCityBrew /
@RedRacerBeer

Central City Brewing Co.

IIIIIIIIIIIIIIIIIIIIIIIIIIIIIIIIIIIIIIIIIIIIIII

I HAVE A distinct memory of the first time I popped open a can of Central City's Red Racer IPA. It was in the summer of 2008, soon after the beer was released. I'd brought a six-pack to a friend's house for a barbecue and when I cracked the can my nose immediately caught a whiff of the pungent hop aroma that is a trademark of this excellent West Coast IPA.

"Holy —," I said to my buddy, Shawn, and held the can out to him. "Take a whiff of this." He waved it under his nose and smiled back at me. My first sip led to another pronouncement of excellence. And on that warm summer evening, I became a full-fledged hophead. Sure, I'd enjoyed hoppy beers before that, but I'd never given myself over to hops, body and soul, before that night.

I'm exaggerating, a little—it wasn't quite a religious experience. But the arrival of Red Racer IPA in its distinctive green can (and the White Ale in its yellow can) that summer marked a turning point in B.C.'s craft beer revolution—that was when Vancouver finally woke up to craft beer, and a big part of that was the success of complex and challenging beers like Central City's Red Racer lineup in attracting new drinkers.

Tap List

RED RACER
INDIA PALE ALE
6.5% ABV | 80 IBU
One of the best IPAS anywhere, this is a hop bomb with glorious citrus-pine aromas and flavours.

RED RACER WHITE ALE
5% ABV | 16 IBU
A spicy, summery wit beer, brewed with coriander seed and dried orange peel.

IMPERIAL IPA
9% ABV | 90 IBU
Bursting with grapefruit, tangerine and tropical fruit flavours balanced with a big malt foundation.

THOR'S HAMMER
BARLEY WINE (seasonal)
11.5% ABV
You can try a bottle-conditioned or bourbon barrel-aged version of this award-winning brew.

Back in 2003 when the Central City brewpub opened as part of a large mall development next to the second-last SkyTrain stop about thirty-five minutes from downtown Vancouver, the big city's beer drinkers barely noticed. Locals didn't exactly come in droves, either. But when the canned beer showed up on the market, beer lovers began converging on the brewpub to sample special brews that were only available there, such as a Rauchbier (smoked beer), Imperial IPA, nitrogenated stout, and an authentic Czech Pilsner.

More styles were released in cans, including an ESB, pumpkin ale and winter ale, each can a different colour but featuring the same eye-catching image of a buxom lass on a retro bicycle. Cask events followed, and Central City's brews began winning awards, including top honours at the 2010 Canadian Brewing Awards, where it won gold medals for its IPA, imperial IPA and barley wine (which also won Beer of the Year), and took home the Brewery of the Year award. Central City was named Canadian Brewery of the Year again in 2012.

Brewmaster Gary Lohin, widely respected as one of B.C.'s best brewers, if not *the* best, is the reason for the success (see "A Passion for Brewing" on page 129). He should get to expand on his reputation even more with the completion of a new 60,000-square-foot, $20-million brewery that will increase Central City's brewing capacity by more than 400 per cent. He has plans for a full-time Cascadian Dark Ale, more IPAs, sour Belgian styles and a barrel-aging program, which should all be available in bottles.

Facts & Figures

OPENED ⟩ *2003* ⊗ **STYLES PRODUCED** ⟩ *6 + seasonals* ⊗
WHERE TO BUY ⟩ *Liquor stores throughout B.C.* ⊗ **ON TAP** ⟩
The brewpub, and throughout Greater Vancouver ⊗
GROWLERS ⟩ *Yes*

www.deadfrog.ca
1-888-856-1055
1-27272 Gloucester Way, Aldergrove
E-MAIL info@deadfrog.ca
TWITTER @deadfrogbrewery

Dead Frog Brewery

||||||||||||||||||||||||||||||||||||||||||||||

I HAVE TO admit that I had a negative attitude about Dead Frog starting, well, right about when they adopted that new name after undergoing a rebranding from their original name, Backwoods Brewing. Not that Backwoods was a better name. It wasn't. But the new name was chosen more as a sales tool than anything else. I believe that craft beer sells itself when it is *good*, not because of how it is marketed. And their beer seemed to be all about marketing, as epitomized by slogans like "Do it froggy style" and "Nothing goes down like a cold Dead Frog." That, and the fact that they chose to use clear-glass bottles (and were even sued by Sleeman Breweries because of it) even though light degrades beer very quickly, which is why most brewers use brown bottles and closed boxes. My grumpiness was only reinforced by some of the styles Dead Frog chose to brew: Pepper Lime, which made me think of Bud Lime; Mandarin Orange, which just confused me; and Christmas Beeracle, which featured cinnamon, nutmeg and ginger—not my style at all.

When I heard the brewery was going to appear on the CBC-TV reality show, *The Big Decision*, I tuned in with skeptical curiosity.

Tap List

PALE ALE
5% ABV | 20 IBU
A solid Northwest pale ale that won't knock your socks off but is a great session beer.

PEPPER LIME LAGER
5% ABV | 12 IBU
A big seller in Alberta, but not as popular in more crafty B.C.

TOASTED COCONUT WIT
5% ABV | 5 IBU
A well-made Belgian wit beer with a tinge of toasted coconut.

FEARLESS IPA
6.5% ABV | 77 IBU
Potent and bitter, but without the citrusy hop aroma it needs to truly be called a West Coast IPA.

The premise of the show was that Jim Treliving, the multimillionaire owner of the Boston Pizza chain, would pick between two businesses in need of his cash. It was Dead Frog Brewery against a Winnipeg manufacturing company. The show made the management team look inept, and painted the brewery as being on its last legs, about to collapse without Jim's help. But not once did they show Jim tasting the beer or talking about what's important in craft beer: ingredients, flavour, experience, innovation, etc. All he wanted to do was reduce the brewery's lineup to four styles and market the hell out of them. It made me think even less of Dead Frog.

But my bad attitude changed when I visited the brewery in the summer of 2012. Meeting the management team in person, I immediately saw their enthusiasm for their beer. The TV show's negative presentation of them had come as a complete surprise, and even though they'd won that episode several months before, they hadn't seen a penny yet, and were still in negotiations with the pizza czar.

Derrick Smith, the president, told me he had finally succeeded in buying out some silent partners and now would have the freedom to direct the brewers to brew more styles he wanted, like a true West Coast IPA. He seems to be putting his money where his mouth is, too, by hiring a couple of respected B.C. brewers and releasing a hop-forward IPA—and in brown bottles no less.

Facts & Figures

OPENED › *1998 (as Backwoods Brewing—renamed in 2006)* ✪
STYLES PRODUCED › *8 + seasonals* ✪ **WHERE TO BUY ›**
Liquor stores throughout B.C. ✪ **ON TAP ›** *Throughout B.C.*
✪ **GROWLERS ›** *No*

**www.missionspringsbrewing
company.com**
604-820-1009
7160 Oliver Street (at Lougheed
Highway), Mission
E-MAIL info@missionsprings
brewingcompany.com
TWITTER @msbcbrewery

Mission Springs Brewing Company

||||||||||||||||||||||||||||||||||||||||||||||

TEN MINUTES EAST of Golden Ears Provincial Park, one of the most popular camping destinations in the Lower Mainland, is the town of Mission, which is home to one of the most interesting brewpubs in the province. Mission Springs Brewing Company opened in 1996 as an expansion to the existing pub there, creating a real destination for beer lovers with a 425-seat family restaurant and a 120-seat adults-only pub.

The place is positively bursting with antiques and memorabilia. There are several antique gas pumps, a moose head and a train whistle. A 1949 Chevy truck is suspended from the ceiling and all the walls are covered in tools, mechanical equipment, hubcaps, musical instruments and old signage of every kind you can imagine: from gas stations, soft drink companies, and cigar and cigarette companies. The tabletops themselves contain artifacts under transparent lacquer, including old spark plugs, licence plates and bullet shells.

The pub is situated in a beautiful spot right above the Fraser River. You can play beach volleyball or basketball there during the summer, and there are numerous beer-related events year-round, including cask

Tap List

BIG CHIEF CREAM ALE

4.5% ABV

A real cream ale, not the Vancouver version—light, creamy and easy-drinking.

BOMBSHELL BLONDE

4.5% ABV

Not particularly memorable as a beer, but it has an incredible label.

**FAT GUY
OATMEAL STOUT**

5.6% ABV

An excellent stout—thick and creamy with a great roasted malt character.

**OLDE SAILOR'S
INDIA PALE ALE**

5.6% ABV

A relatively tame English-style IPA.

nights and a big Craftoberfest celebration every fall with a special Oktoberfest-style beer on tap and German food on the menu.

Speaking of beer, the on-site brewery produces a solid assortment, and the pub also serves guest taps from other leading B.C. craft brewers. All in all, Mission Springs is a great spot to enjoy craft beer. The only difficulty is in getting there. If you're coming from Vancouver, you'll need a car, so bring a designated driver with an interest in antiques and collectibles. Then, he or she can be occupied by the eclectic collection while the passengers enjoy the beer.

Facts & Figures

OPENED ‣ *1996* ✪ **STYLES PRODUCED** ‣ *4 + seasonals* ✪ **WHERE TO BUY** ‣ *Mission Springs private liquor store and select private stores in Greater Vancouver* ✪ **ON TAP** ‣ *The brewpub* ✪ **GROWLERS** ‣ *Yes*

www.oldyalebrewing.com
604-392-2011
4-7965 Venture Place, Chilliwack
E-MAIL info@oldyalebrewing.com
TWITTER @oldyalebrewing

Old Yale Brewing Company

||||||||||||||||||||||||||||||||||||||||||||

EX-AIR FORCE PILOT Larry Caza got interested in beer when he was stationed in Goose Bay, Newfoundland, thanks to other international pilots who introduced him to beers like Budwar from the Czech Republic and Sierra Nevada Pale Ale, one of the flagship beers of the American craft beer movement. Back home in Chilliwack after he retired from the military, Caza began home brewing and then made the leap to professional brewing when he opened Old Yale Brewing in 2000. (It's interesting to note that Caza purchased his original brewing equipment from Deschutes Brewery in Bend, Oregon, which has grown into one of the Pacific Northwest's premier craft breweries.)

Although his beer was well respected and sold reasonably well, Caza says the business struggled and lost money, partially because of a lack of interest in craft beer in the local community, but also because the original location had logistical issues with a limited capacity. By the fall of 2010, he couldn't keep it going, so he shut the doors and put it up for sale. A year later, Old Yale reopened in a new, better location with three new co-owners. Caza is still in charge of the brewing, but now, along with an injection of new capital

Tap List

CHILLIWACK BLONDE
5% ABV
A flavourful, easy-drinking blonde ale.

OLD YALE PALE ALE
5% ABV
A tasty pale ale with a solid malt base and some nice hop character.

SASQUATCH STOUT
5% ABV
This is a thick, robust stout that will keep you warm even if you aren't covered with hair.

SERGEANT'S IPA
5.5% ABV
A flavourful English-style IPA with a big floral hop flavour.

and a new canning line, he has three excited, beer-loving business partners.

The newly resurrected Old Yale Brewing Company brews all of the original styles, although they have been repackaged with snazzy new labels. Caza hopes to add some seasonal styles, too: "The more seasonals you brew, the more beer you sell," he believes.

Chilliwack is Bible Belt country, and Caza admits that craft beer was a tough sell in the area when he first opened. Locals didn't embrace it initially, he says, but "it's vastly different now. We're on tap everywhere now." Local pubs are buying the beer, and restaurants and bars in Vancouver are picking it up, too. The brewery's range also extends east to Harrison Hot Springs and Hope.

The original brewery only sold beer in kegs for draft accounts or in 650 mL bombers, but part of the new brewery's vision was to add cans to the lineup, giving them some more sales options and opening them up to the prime camping and barbecuing market. After all, nearby Cultus Lake is one of the Lower Mainland's most popular summer spots.

Facts & Figures

OPENED › *2000 (closed in 2010 and reopened in 2011)* ✪
STYLES PRODUCED › *4 + seasonals* ✪ **WHERE TO BUY ›**
Liquor stores throughout B.C. ✪ **ON TAP ›** *Chilliwack, Harrison Hot Springs, Hope and Vancouver* ✪ **GROWLERS ›** *No*

BREWER'S GOLD

The History of Hop Growing
in the Fraser Valley

....

ONCE UPON A TIME, hops were a major agricultural crop in British Columbia, attracting thousands of migrant workers during harvest each August and September. The earliest cultivation of this vigorous plant in B.C. dates back to 1862 when farmers in Saanich, just north of Victoria, began growing hops to sell to local brewers. A shortage in other countries allowed Saanich hop farmers to make big profits in the 1880s, which created interest among farmers in other parts of the province, including Squamish, Kelowna, Vernon and around Chilliwack in the Fraser Valley.

The Saanich industry died out soon after because of a hop louse infestation, and farmers everywhere else except the Fraser Valley turned to other crops. But in the Chilliwack area, the industry grew and grew until the 1940s when nearly two thousand acres were under cultivation there, with four thousand people employed during the harvest each year. Temporary towns were struck among the hop fields, with stores, a dance hall and other amenities, and tents or cabins provided by the farmers. Among the pickers were First Nations people, as well as members of the Chinese, Japanese and Mennonite communities. Entire families would go to work in the hop fields: the men would take down the hop bines and the children and women would pick the hop flowers. Pickers were paid by weight—the best could harvest up to 200 pounds in a day.

At its peak, the Fraser Valley represented the largest hop growing region in the entire British Commonwealth. But after World War II, the industry began shrinking, and in the 1950s, the farms began using mechanized pickers, which ended the need for such a large number of workers. Inexorably, fewer and fewer farmers chose to grow hops until the last of the great Fraser Valley hop farms closed down in 1997.

Thanks in part to the efforts of Crannóg Ales' co-founder Rebecca Kneen (see pg. 156), there has been a resurgence in hops cultivation in B.C., this time focused mainly on organic production. Now, it is estimated that there are at least six organic hops farms in B.C., along with other conventional (non-organic) farms, including the Sartori Cedar Ranch in Chilliwack, which supplies the fresh hops for Driftwood Brewery's Sartori Harvest IPA and also sells hops to other breweries, including, rumour has it, Molson-Coors.

For more information on this interesting part of B.C. history, check out the online exhibit, *Brewer's Gold*, at www.chilliwack-museum.ca.

www.russellbeer.com
604-599-1190
202-13018 Eightieth Avenue, Surrey
E-MAIL cheers@russellbeer.com
TWITTER @Russell_Beer

Russell Brewing Co.

||||||||||||||||||||||||||||||||||||||||||

FOUNDED IN 1995 by Arthur Russell and his sons Peter and Mark, Russell Brewing remained a small operation that supplied a loyal following with its amber and cream ales for several years. Then, in 2004, the Russells approached one of their most dedicated customers, Andrew Harris, who ran a restaurant that had served Russell beer right from the start—he bought the second keg the brewery ever sold—and offered to sell him the brewery. Harris took the idea to his own father, Brian, who had decades of experience setting up and running tech companies around the world, and the Harrises decided to buy the operation. Brian, who became CEO, saw a chance to grow the company into a national brand the way Sleeman Breweries had. Andrew, president and COO, was more interested in brewing great beer for the B.C. market.

That split in vision sums up the public perception of Russell Brewing perfectly. Depending on how you look at the company, you could easily argue that it isn't a craft brewery at all—or that it's one of B.C.'s best craft brewers. Its Session Series is uninteresting, apart from the flagship cream ale*. It also brews Rocky Mountain Pilsner to compete with big brands like Kokanee, Blue and

Tap List

BLACK DEATH PORTER
6.5% ABV | 53 IBU
Thick and black as night with a strong roasted malt character and a deep bitterness.

BLOOD ALLEY BITTER
5.5% ABV | 50 IBU
Named for a notorious Gastown laneway, this is truly an extra bitter bitter. Exceptional.

IP'EH!
6.5% ABV | 53 IBU
A very good British-style IPA—malty and hoppy.

A WEE ANGRY SCOTCH ALE
6.5% ABV | 30 IBU
A strong, dark ale with a slightly smoky character thanks to the use of peated malt.

Bud, and a Lemon Ale and Lime Lager, mainly for the Alberta market, where these styles still sell well. For a time, the brewery also brewed BC Lions Lager for BC Place Stadium, but Andrew Harris told me they pulled out after their first season when they discovered the tap lines hadn't been cleaned for months.

On the other side of the spectrum is their Brewmaster Series of excellent, challenging brews that are very popular in the craft beer community. The regular lineup there includes a solid IPA, potent porter, unbelievable bitter and a magnificently malty scotch ale, as well as special one-offs like the 6-26 Anniversary Scotch Ale that was aged in bourbon barrels; Nectar of the Gods Wheat Wine Ale; Hop Therapy, a potent double IPA; and Rick August Russian Imperial Stout, a collaboration with the winner of a homebrew contest. They have also collaborated with James Walton of Storm Brewing to produce Big Smoke Ale, and regularly act as the brewer for the Vancouver Craft Beer Week Collaboration beer.

Taken on its own, Russell's Brewmaster Series would easily merit consideration as one of the best arrays of craft beer in B.C., but the company's split personality is confusing and discouraging to consumers. It's almost as if the brewery needs to be split in two, but that isn't about to happen as it is a publicly traded corporation which also owns Fort Garry Brewing in Winnipeg.

* Russell's cream ale is not really a cream ale—just like the cream ale originally brewed by Shaftebury or R&B's Raven Cream Ale, it is dark and smooth, more a British mild than anything else. Call it a Vancouver cream ale.

....

Facts & Figures

OPENED ‣ *1995 (new ownership as of 2004)* ✪ **STYLES PRODUCED** ‣ *10 + seasonals* ✪ **WHERE TO BUY** ‣ *Liquor stores throughout B.C.* ✪ **ON TAP** ‣ *Pubs and restaurants throughout the Lower Mainland* ✪ **GROWLERS** ‣ *No*

BEST BEERS

Richmond,
Surrey & Fraser Valley

••••••••••••••••••••••••

Big Ridge Brewpub Wrath of Khan Belgian IPA
A seasonal beer so good it'd make Captain Kirk strut and fret and call out for more: "Khan!! Khan!!!"

Central City Brewing Red Racer IPA
Quite possibly the best IPA in Canada, certainly the best in a can (and thus the best camping beer in history).

Dead Frog Brewery Fearless IPA
A big step in the right direction for Dead Frog.

Old Yale Brewing Sasquatch Stout
A thick, black, rich stout that will put some hair on ... well, all over your body!

Russell Brewing Blood Alley Bitter
Just as a vampire's thirst for blood is never-ending, this excellent bitter will leave you craving more and more.

THOMPSON-OKANAGAN

AT THE BREWERY	DRAFT	FOOD	GROWLERS	BOTTLE SALES	TOURS	BEDS
Barley Mill Brewpub	★	★		★	★	
Barley Station Brewhouse	★	★	★	★	★	
Cannery Brewing			★	★	★	
Crannóg Ales			★		★	
Firehall Brewery			★		★	
Freddy's Brewpub	★	★	★		★	
Noble Pig Brewpub	★	★	★		★	
Ridge Brewpub	★	★				★
Tin Whistle Brewing			★	★	★	
Tree Brewing			★	★	★	

CRAFT BEER
IN WINE COUNTRY

....

WHEN YOU HEAR the word "Okanagan," you probably think of wine country. But the region also has a well-established and diverse craft beer community, with five breweries and five brewpubs stretching from Osoyoos in the arid south right up to Salmon Arm in the north and then west to Kamloops. The Okanagan is also home to a clutch of five small distilleries, which are part of the nascent craft distillery movement that is beginning to pick up steam here in British Columbia (see "Craft Distilleries" on page 163). The distilling industry in the Okanagan has a lot to do with the abundance of fruit grown alongside the grapes—and most of the craft brewers in the region also feature fruit prominently in their lineups.

Penticton's beer scene is the most developed with two strong breweries, Cannery and Tin Whistle, a brewpub, and the Kettle Valley Station, a local pub that offers craft beer from the region and elsewhere. Penticton also hosts the Okanagan Fest-of-Ale each April, a two-day event that showcases breweries from the region alongside their colleagues from elsewhere in Canada and the United States.

One of the things I love about the Okanagan's craft beer scene is the wide range of styles and approaches—something that reflects the region's great variation in geography and ecology, from the desert-like southern Osoyoos/Similka-meen area to the lake-studded north Okanagan, and the drier, rugged terrain around Kamloops. That varied landscape is reflected in the breweries themselves—balancing out Tree's regional dominance in Kelowna is the Firehall Brewery in Oliver, one of the smallest and newest operations in the province. Among the array of brewpubs salted across the scene are some good ones, some bad ones, and one that might just be the best in B.C.: the Noble Pig in Kamloops, a city that is not known for craft beer. Finally, there is the unconventional Crannóg Ales, unlike any other brewery in Canada.

All in all, there is definitely a case to be made for drinking craft beer in wine country.

www.barleymillpub.com
250-493-8000
2460 Skaha Lake Road, Penticton

Barley Mill Brewpub

Tap List

MUSTANG PALE ALE
5% ABV
A basic pale ale, not very
complex or challenging.

NITE MARE BROWN ALE
5% ABV
A brown ale with a bit of
flavour, though not much
body.

THE BARLEY MILL'S Tudor-style architecture stands out in downtown Penticton. Inside, the two-storey brewpub is very comfortable with a large restaurant downstairs and an upstairs bistro that features a large collection of sports memorabilia, including a Gordie Howe hockey jersey. While you're up there, ask for a tour of the tiny brewhouse, one of the smallest I've ever seen.

Unfortunately, the beer selection is not very inspiring. The standard menu has four very light, bland beers—two ales and two lagers that are virtually identical in flavour and appearance—and a slightly more flavourful brown ale. Hopefully, the rotating seasonal brew will be more interesting: it may be the only chance the brewer gets to experiment a little.

Facts & Figures

OPENED ‣ *1998* ✪ **STYLES PRODUCED** ‣ *5 + seasonals* ✪ **WHERE TO BUY** ‣ *In cans from the connected Barley Mill liquor store* ✪ **ON TAP** ‣ *At the brewpub* ✪ **GROWLERS** ‣ *No*

OKANAGAN
FEST-OF-ALE

....

A two-day festival held in Penticton every April

THE OKANAGAN FEST-OF-ALE is the biggest beer event held in central B.C. each year. Based in Penticton in the heart of wine country, it showcases all of the area's breweries as well as others from elsewhere in B.C. and the rest of Canada.

This is a popular Friday–Saturday event that is held in the local convention centre. It can be a bit of a drink-up for some attendees, but it's also a great way to check out the beer scene in the Okanagan. I recommend heading out a day or two early so you can visit some of the breweries and craft distilleries directly (or I guess you can check out a winery or two if you're into that). One local wine tour operator, Grape Friends, operates a "Barley, Hops and Spirits" tour that is a great way to get a taste of the region. (Check out www.grapefriendsloungeandtours.com for more information.)

And if you are in Penticton when the festival isn't on, drop by the Kettle Valley Station Pub. Connected to the Ramada Inn and Suites, it is a great place to enjoy all the best local beers, as well as interesting brands from around the world.

www.fest-of-ale.bc.ca

www.barleystation.com
250-832-0999
20 Shuswap Street SE
Salmon Arm
E-MAIL bstation@telus.net

Barley Station Brew Pub

Tap List

BUSHWACKER BROWN ALE
4.7% ABV | 24 IBU
Even more robust than it looks with a chocolaty nuttiness and some roasted barley character.

ESB (seasonal)
5% ABV
An excellent ESB with a great balance of malt and hop bitterness.

SAM MCGUIRE'S PALE ALE
4.6% ABV | 45 IBU
A solid Northwest pale ale with some surprising hop bitterness, although with virtually no hop aroma.

TALKING DOG WIT
4.9% ABV | 12 IBU
An excellent Belgian wit with subtle tones of coriander and orange peel.

|||||||||||||||||||||||||||||||||||||||||||||

RIGHT ON A slow stretch of the Trans-Canada Highway in Salmon Arm, a small city on the shore of picturesque Shuswap Lake, the Barley Station Brew Pub has one of the best locations you could ask for. Owner Stu Bradford says that he and his wife, Kathy, decided to open the place in 2006 in response to local demand for a brewpub, and they named the operation after its location—a building originally built as a replica of an old-fashioned train station.

I'll admit that when I dropped in as part of my Craft Beer Odyssey around B.C., I was not expecting to be impressed by the beer. I'd already visited two other brewpubs in the Okanagan region that, unfortunately, do not make very interesting beer, so I figured the Barley Station would be similarly disappointing. Happily, my expectations were turned upside down. Brewer Damon Robson, who took the reins from brewpub consultant and guru Don Moore, makes a solid range of five main beers along with some rotating seasonals. Serious hopheads will not be satisfied here since there isn't a regular West Coast IPA in the lineup, but I could have contentedly sipped the Bushwacker Brown Ale or the seasonal ESB all day if I didn't have places to go and people to see.

The brewpub recently started canning its beer for off-sales, and they also have a growler program in place. The menu is diverse and even includes food-and-beer pairing suggestions, while the interior of the pub is very comfortable and spacious with a large patio.

Facts & Figures

OPENED ‣ *2006* ⊗ **STYLES PRODUCED** ‣ *5 + seasonals* ⊗ **WHERE TO BUY** ‣ *In cans and growlers at the brewpub* ⊗ **ON TAP** ‣ *The brewpub* ⊗ **GROWLERS** ‣ *Yes*

AN OKANAGAN ORIGINAL: ONCE GREAT, NOW JUST BIG

Okanagan Spring Brewery

·······················

BACK IN 1992, the first job I had after I moved to B.C. was as a box office clerk at the Belfry Theatre in Victoria. I worked evenings for the first couple years, putting the shows in and then tallying up the ticket sales before selling subscriptions or tickets for future events during intermission. After intermission, I'd close up the ticket window and, more often than not, head across the street to the George & Dragon Pub (now the Fernwood Inn) for a pint of Okanagan Spring Extra Special Pale Ale. Once the curtain was down, co-workers from the backstage side of the theatre would show up along with the actors, and more pints or pitchers of OK Spring would follow.

We served Okanagan Spring beer at the theatre, too, so I drank a lot of it in those days, and happily. Back in the late 1980s and 1990s, Okanagan Spring brewed some great beer. In addition to their standard pale ale and lager, they had a solid stout and some specialty styles, like Old Munich Wheat. And back then, they bottled their beer in stubbies, which were very cool.

The brewery was founded by Buko von Krosigk and Jakob Tobler in 1985. The story goes that they were disappointed with the mainstream beers in Canada after moving to the Okanagan from Germany. Even though they didn't have any brewing experience, they bought an old fruit-packing house in Vernon and turned it into a brewery, hiring a friend from Germany, Raimund Kalinowsky, to join them as their original brewmaster. Tobler's son Stefan mentored under Kalinowsky and then studied brewing in Germany before taking over as brewmaster himself in 1989.

Originally, OK Spring brewed German-style lagers, but they quickly found there was more of a market for ales so they switched their focus in that direction. They also realized that they needed to sell their beer outside of the Okanagan and aggressively marketed themselves in the Lower Mainland and on Vancouver Island. This pattern of growth continued until they had become B.C.'s largest "microbrewery" and were subsequently purchased by Sleeman Breweries in 1996, which itself was bought by Sapporo ten years later.

In the mid-'90s, I definitely noticed the quality of OK Spring's beer diminish. They were quickly surpassed by newer craft breweries arriving on the B.C. scene. It seems as if growth on the scale Okanagan Spring underwent resulted directly in a toning down of flavour in an attempt to make their beer more palatable to a wider audience. The same sort of thing happened with Big Rock Brewery in Alberta, and now, the two breweries' products are very similar to me: wannabe craft beer that just doesn't make it in the flavour department.

www.cannerybrewing.com
250-493-2723
112-1475 Fairview Road, Penticton
E-MAIL info@cannerybrewing.com
TWITTER @CanneryBrewing

Cannery Brewing

||||||||||||||||||||||||||||||||||||||||||||||

Tap List

ANARCHIST AMBER ALE

5.5% ABV

Named for nearby Anarchist Mountain, this is a nonconformist amber ale with a nice dose of West Coast hops.

NARAMATA NUT BROWN ALE

5.5% ABV

This velvety smooth brown ale is named for the tiny town of Naramata, famous for its many wineries. And now for this great beer.

SQUIRE SCOTCH ALE

6.5% ABV

Few brewers brew scotch ales. Fewer brew them this well. Deep caramel colour with a sweet, smoked malt flavour.

APRICOT WHEAT ALE (seasonal)

5% ABV

Reflecting the fruit-growing culture of the Okanagan, this wheat ale bursts with apricot flavour. Perfect for a summer patio.

RON AND PATT DYCK were well-established restaurateurs in 2000 with twenty-three years of experience operating the Country Squire restaurant in the town of Naramata just north of Penticton when their chef, an avid homebrewer named Terry Schofer, told them about some brewing equipment he'd heard was for sale. Ron says he loved the idea of running a brewery right from the start, but he had to persuade a lot of people to agree with him: his wife, his banker, other business colleagues, and so on. He persisted and won out.

They decided to set up shop in the historic Aylmer fruit and vegetable cannery in Penticton, but it was a major challenge just getting the brewing equipment into this non-traditional space. And then there was a steep learning curve setting it up and making it operational. They finally brewed their first batch of beer, Naramata Nut Brown Ale, which is still one of their best sellers, on April 1, 2001 (no fooling). At first, Cannery only sold its beer in kegs to local restaurants and bars, but then it added an 8.5-litre "party pig" mini-keg which became very popular with the locals, especially in the summer months.

When they did start bottling, Cannery first used a clear-glass one-litre bottle with a re-closable, Grolsch-style cap. Eventually they made the move to the industry standard 650 mL bomber bottle and when economics allowed it in 2006, they added a canning line to their operation. They were one of the first B.C. breweries to offer a mixed pack, the "Cannery Collection," which includes two cans each of Naramata Nut Brown, Cannery IPA and Anarchist Amber Ale. Recently, they joined the growler craze—theirs is the only clear glass growler I've seen. I guess the issue of UV degradation which keeps most brewers from using clear glass isn't a problem with a growler since it is meant to be consumed within a few days of purchase.

Now, you will find Cannery beers on tap everywhere in the Penticton area and throughout the Okanagan. They have developed a deservedly solid reputation for their beers and have even come full circle by co-hosting beer dinners at the Naramata Inn's highly respected restaurant—previously known as the Country Squire.

Facts & Figures

OPENED ⟩ *2001* ✪ **STYLES PRODUCED** ⟩ *11+ seasonals* ✪ **WHERE TO BUY** ⟩ *At the brewery and liquor stores throughout B.C.* ✪ **ON TAP** ⟩ *Throughout the Okanagan* ✪ **GROWLERS** ⟩ *Yes*

www.crannogales.com
250-675-6847
706 Elson Road, Sorrento
E-MAIL brewery@crannogales.com

Crannóg Ales

||||||||||||||||||||||||||||||||||||||||||||

CANADA'S ONE AND ONLY certified organic farmhouse brewery, Crannóg Ales is a truly unique place that any B.C. beer lover should visit at least once. While Crannóg's exceptional beers are available on tap in much of southwestern and central B.C., it's another thing to go directly to the source and see what goes into it. But plan ahead: the brewery offers public tours by reservation only on Fridays and Saturdays in the summer.

Founders Brian MacIsaac and Rebecca Kneen left Vancouver to move to this ten-acre farm just above Shuswap Lake, halfway between Kamloops and Salmon Arm, in 2000. They built much of the brewery themselves, converting some of the farm buildings that were already there and using brewhouse equipment from B.C.'s original microbrewery, Horseshoe Bay Brewing. Today, they brew ales in a traditional English/Irish style, including the very popular Back Hand of God Stout, Red Branch Irish Ale, Insurrection IPA, and Gael's Blood Potato Ale, which is brewed with organic potatoes.

The brewers planted their own organic hops in 2000 and began harvesting for production two years later. At that time, organic hops were only available from New Zealand,

Tap List

**BACK
HAND OF GOD STOUT**
5.2% ABV | 18 IBU
Crannóg's flagship beer—a dry stout that isn't heavy but has lots of flavour.

**GAEL'S
BLOOD POTATO ALE**
5.2% ABV | 48 IBU
An Irish red ale with a smooth, rich body. Very tasty with quite a hop bite on top of a solid malt (and potato!) foundation.

INSURRECTION IPA
5.4% ABV | 54 IBU
A lightweight in terms of alcohol, this IPA holds its own against the big boys.

**POOKA
CHERRY ALE** (seasonal)
5% ABV
A summer seasonal lightly hopped ale brewed with four hundred pounds of cherries from Crannóg's own trees or a local farm.

and apart from the costs and environmental footprint of shipping over that distance, Crannóg was also concerned about relying on only one source. Hops were once a major crop in B.C., but the industry all but died out by the 1980s (see "Brewer's Gold" on page 140). Once Crannóg had a viable crop growing, they found there was a lot of interest from other B.C. farmers and brewers, too. With government assistance, Kneen produced a manual on small-scale hop production and made it publicly available. They also began selling hop rhizomes (root stock for others to plant), single-handedly spearheading a revival in organic hop growing in Canada. As of 2012, there were at least six farms growing hops for commercial sales in B.C., as well as several more in Ontario and Quebec.

On only ten acres, the brewery doesn't have very much room to grow barley; besides, the climate isn't ideal for grains. However, Crannóg does use berries, plums and other fruit that grows on the property in its beers. And in the cycle of organic farming, the spent grains are fed to the pigs (who especially love the potatoes from the Gael's Blood brew). They also have sheep that keep the grass down in the hopyards and love to eat the leaves from the hop bines after they are picked.

Most aspects of this organic farm and brewery seem to go full-circle that way, including the brewery itself. After all, as John Mitchell, the founder of Horseshoe Bay Brewing, pointed out when he visited Crannóg several years back: the equipment from Canada's first microbrewery is now being used by the country's first all-organic brewery.

Facts & Figures

OPENED › *2000* ✿ **STYLES PRODUCED ›** *4 + seasonals* ✿ **WHERE TO BUY ›** *In growlers or party pigs from the brewery* ✿ **ON TAP ›** *The Shuswap, Okanagan, Greater Vancouver and Vancouver Island* ✿ **GROWLERS ›** *Yes*

SISTERS
OF THE HOP

Leading Women of B.C.'s
Craft Beer Industry

....

FOR MOST of its history, beer was mainly the domain of women who brewed it for consumption by their families. Starting in the 1600s when beer began to be commercialized, however, brewing became a predominantly male occupation. And in the twentieth century, beer drinking came to be seen as a male pre-occupation, at least in North American popular culture. But as the craft beer revolution has overtaken North America, women have returned to the beer industry as brewers, managers and, of course, consumers.

Here in B.C., we have a small but strong contingent of female brewers, including Rebecca Kneen, the co-owner of Crannóg Ales. Claire Connolly was the brewer at Big River Brewpub for several years and is now striking out on her own by starting Dogwood Brewing. At Spinnakers, Kala Hadfield, daughter of founder Paul Hadfield, grew up in the brewpub, and is now a brewer there. She is responsible for some of its hoppier beers, including the excellent Northwest Ale. Her sister Carly, though not a brewer, is evangelizing the message of craft beer in the heart of Kokanee country as co-owner of the Lion's Head Pub in Robson. Nelson Brewing and R&B Brewing also have female brewers.

There are also several B.C. breweries that are run by husband-and-wife teams, including Salt Spring Island Ales, Mt. Begbie,

Arrowhead, Wolf, Powell Street and Bridge. Howe Sound has a unique brother-and-sister management team, with Leslie Fenn as CEO. Townsite Brewing was the brainchild of Karen Skadsheim, and brewery manager Chloe Smith also hopes to brew alongside husband Cédric Dauchot—once their baby gives her the freedom to do so.

The Pink Boots Society is an international organization that aims to "empower women beer professionals to advance their careers in the beer industry through education." Pink Boots also has a consumer arm called Barley's Angels, and Vancouver is host to the Pink Pints chapter of that group, which is run by Lundy Dale, who is herself a leading female figure in the craft beer scene. She was one of the founding members of the CAMRA Vancouver branch, then its president, and also stood as president of CAMRA B.C. After working as a craft beer expert at one of the city's private liquor stores, she took a job in marketing at R&B Brewing in 2012. (Follow her on Twitter @PinkPints for information on events.)

Vancouver Craft Beer Week holds a Sisters of the Tap event each year which features B.C. breweries with women in brewing or management roles. And there is a very active Sisters of the Tap group in Victoria, with regular events that include brewery tours, food-beer pairing seminars, and beer style explorations. Check out sistersofthetap.tumblr.com for more information.

www.firehallbrewery.com
778-439-2337
6077 Main Street, Oliver
E-MAIL firehallbrewery@gmail.com
TWITTER @FirehallBrewery

Firehall Brewery

|||||||||||||||||||||||||||||||||||||||||||||||

Tap List

HOLY SMOKE STOUT

4.5% ABV | 24 IBU

This is a rather unique beer in B.C.: a dry stout melded with German Rauchbier (smoked beer), which uses barley malt smoked over a beechwood fire. You'll be pleasantly surprised by the smoky flavour.

STOKED EMBER ALE

4.9% ABV | 31 IBU

A traditional English-style bitter (amber ale) with a bit of an extra Northwest hop zing.

THE TOWN OF OLIVER, halfway between Penticton and Osoyoos in the south Okanagan, calls itself the Wine Capital of Canada, but among all those vineyards and wineries you can also visit one of B.C.'s newest breweries, Firehall Brewery, which opened in April 2012. The tiny microbrewery is run by a twenty-five-year-old local musician named Sid Ruhland who pours his enthusiasm and energy into every batch of craft beer.

Ruhland grew up in Oliver, then went away to school in Kelowna, where he says he was too young to buy beer, but not to brew it in his dorm room. Later, he spent a year abroad based in Austria where he travelled far and wide in search of beer. After graduating from business school, he decided to apply his brewing skills and business knowledge to opening this brewery.

The brewery is based in Oliver's original firehall, which was built in 1948 for the town's volunteer fire department. After a new firehall was built in 2003, the building was renovated to house a restaurant space upstairs, which is now called the Firehall Bistro. The brewery is in the basement.

As Ruhland showed me around the small brewhouse, I noticed that each of his pieces of equipment had an unusual name. The brew kettle was "BB King," and the hot liquor tank, "Hendrix." The fermenters were "Led" and "Zeppelin," another one read "Floyd." In the cold room, Ruhland saw me read the names on the two aging tanks, "Crosby" and "Stills," and with a wry smile between his thick muttonchop sideburns, he pointed to the empty half of the room. "Can you guess who we'll put in here one day?"

Music is a big part of life for Ruhland and his friends, many of whom help out at the brewery on a volunteer basis, no doubt in exchange for the occasional sample now and then. They believe music and beer go hand in hand; they have already staged a series of four concerts behind the brewery in the Firehall Bistro Back Alley Concert Series.

In their first year of operation, Firehall Brewery focused on just two styles: Stoked Ember Ale and Holy Smoke Stout. The stout, especially, is quite interesting: a hybrid stout brewed with added German smoked malt. Both are delicious beers.

Drop by the "hydration station" tasting room at the brewery for a chat and a sample—Sid is always ready with a smile and story. Or visit on a summer night for what I'm sure would be a great concert.

Facts & Figures

OPENED ▸ 2012 ✪ **STYLES PRODUCED ▸** 3 ✪ **WHERE TO BUY ▸** In growlers at the brewery ✪ **ON TAP ▸** Oliver ✪ **GROWLERS ▸** Yes

www.mccurdybowl.com
250-491-2695
948 McCurdy Road, Kelowna

Freddy's Brewpub

Tap List

HONEY RIDGE ALE

5% ABV

Very light in body, this honey ale is tinged with coriander for a bit of a zesty kick.

LORD NELSON PALE ALE

5% ABV

The most hopped beer on tap, but still less than 20 IBUS—an easy-drinking pale ale.

‖‖

FREDDY'S IS A bit hard to find, part of a bowling alley on the edge of a suburban mall and, to be honest, its beer isn't that exciting. But if you can arrange a tour with brewer Jack Clark, it's definitely worth a visit. Clark is very entertaining and knowledgeable, bringing thirty years of anecdotes from his time working for Labatt in various capacities. He says he had no interest in microbrewing while he worked at Labatt, but since he took this part-time job to keep busy in his retirement, he has learned a lot—and developed a taste for darker, hoppier beers.

Unfortunately, you won't find many of those on tap here since the owners believe their customers aren't interested. Then again, Clark says the one time he brewed a hoppy IPA (at about 65 IBUS), "I was surprised how well it sold." Funny that. Good beer always sells.

Facts & Figures

OPENED ▸ *2001* ✪ **STYLES PRODUCED ▸** *5 + seasonals* ✪ **WHERE TO BUY ▸** *In growlers at the brewpub* ✪ **ON TAP ▸** *The brewpub* ✪ **GROWLERS ▸** *Yes*

CRAFT
DISTILLERIES

....

FOLLOWING IN the footsteps of the craft beer revolution is a new movement of craft distilleries that has started to gain momentum in B.C. since the first, Okanagan Spirits, opened in 2004. These "microdistilleries" seem to face many of the problems that microbreweries did in the early years, mainly highly restrictive government regulations that make it difficult for them to connect directly with their customers. For instance, when I toured Pemberton Distillery in 2012, owner/distiller Tyler Schramm told me that 75 per cent of the price of one of his bottles of gin or vodka is tax. He also said he is not allowed to deliver his products directly to local restaurants or bars. Rather, the restaurant has to order a bottle through the nearest government liquor store, which is in Whistler, a half-hour drive away, and wait for it to be shipped there from the LDB warehouse in Vancouver. Hopefully, these sort of silly regulations will soon be relaxed following a set of changes to provincial liquor laws announced in early 2013.

Often, these distilleries were founded on the basis of utilizing a surplus local crop, whether it was organic potatoes in Pemberton or leftover fruit in the Okanagan, but the other inspiration seems to be the chance to craft something unique or unusual, such as absinthe or aquavit. Most offer tours and tastings, and you should be able to buy their products directly at the distilleries, or in some cases, in liquor stores. Check the websites for full details.

Dubh Glas Distillery

39036 Ninety-Seventh Street, Oliver

250-486-7529

www.thedubhglasdistillery.com

Grant Stevely hopes to produce single malt whisky in the heart of wine country.

Island Spirits Distillery

4605 Roburn Road, Hornby Island

250-335-0630

www.islandspirits.ca

Makers of Phrog gin and vodka located on beautiful Hornby Island, "Hawaii of the North."

Long Table Distillery

1451 Hornby Street, Vancouver

604-266-0177

www.longtabledistillery.com

Vancouver's first urban craft distillery. The vodka is smooth and silky, and the gin is particularly excellent: big juniper and citrus flavours.

Maple Leaf Spirits

1386 Carmi Avenue, Penticton

250-493-0180

www.mapleleafspirits.ca

German-born Jorg Engel produces fruit liqueurs and brandies, maple liqueur, and award-winning "skinny" (grappa). Arrange a visit and be sure to ask him to demonstrate his parrot trick.

Okanagan Spirits (Two locations)

2920 Twenth-Eighth Avenue, Vernon

250-549-3120

267 Bernard Avenue, Kelowna

778-484-5174

www.okanagansprits.com

B.C.'s original craft distillery, now with two locations, produces a wide variety of fruit liqueurs and brandies, as well as absinthe, gin and grappa.

Pemberton Distillery
1954 Venture Place, Pemberton
604-894-0222
www.pembertondistillery.ca
Tyler and Lorien Schramm opened their distillery in 2009, making vodka from local, organic potatoes, as well as gin, brandy and fruit elixirs. Whisky coming soon.

Shelter Point Distillery
4650 Regent Road, Campbell River
778-420-2200
Shelter Point's single malt whisky will be available beginning in 2014.

Urban Distilleries
6-325 Bay Avenue, Kelowna
778-478-0939
www.urbandistilleries.ca
Mike Urban produces the Spirit Bear line of vodka and gin, as well as Urban whisky and rum.

Victoria Spirits
6170 Old West Saanich Road, Victoria
250-544-8217
www.victoriaspirits.com
Victoria Spirits is a family operation best known for Victoria Gin, a premium gin that has been getting lots of attention.

www.thenoblepig.ca
778-471-5999
650 Victoria Street, Kamloops
E-MAIL meaghan@thenoblepig.ca

The Noble Pig Brewhouse

Tap List

BELGIUM PEPPERED ALE

5.5% ABV

A Belgian saison or farmhouse ale using yeast from a Trappist brewery and added Sechuan peppers.

EMPRESS OF INDIA IMPERIAL RYE IPA (seasonal)

8.5% ABV | 100 IBU

Wow! Make the trip to Kamloops when this is on tap. It's incredible. With 20% rye in the mash.

KILT LIFTER SCOTCH ALE (seasonal)

11% ABV | 18 IBU

A strong Scottish ale released on Robbie Burns Day each year that is amplified with the addition of Highland Park scotch and cellar-conditioned for five months. Simply incredible.

TWIGS & BERRIES (seasonal)

4.8% ABV | 9 IBU

A Belgian fruit beer using blueberries, blackberries and raspberries, fermented with a Chimay yeast that dates back to 1989.

||||||||||||||||||||||||||||||||||||||||||||||

KAMLOOPS ISN'T EXACTLY known for its thriving craft beer scene, although it has been home to a microbrewery of sorts since 1995. That brewery, originally named Bear Brewing, took over the Bowen Island and Whistler Brewing brands in 2001 and then itself was bought by Alberta's Big Rock Brewery in 2003 as part of an expansion into the B.C. market. Big Rock sold the brewery to a Vancouver company in 2005 and it was renamed Kamloops Brewery, with the focus being the Whistler brand, in preparation for the Winter Olympics, and the Bowen Island brand, a budget craft imitator. In other words, the beer brewed in Kamloops hasn't really been intended for the local market since back before the turn of the millennium.

But the Noble Pig Brewhouse, which opened there in 2010, has changed all that in a few short years. The Pig, as locals call it, is easily one of the best brewpubs in B.C., maybe *the* best. The man behind the Noble Pig is David Beardsell, who trained in Germany and the UK in the 1980s and then worked at Okanagan Spring Brewery in the early '90s before opening and running Bear Brewing for several years. He thought he'd retired from brewing when he sold Bear to

Big Rock, and he took his family on the road in an old bus for two and a half years.

But then the old itch returned and he decided to open a brewpub, which he says is "the most rewarding way to make beer" compared to his experiences at big breweries. He loves the variety available to him—he brewed twenty-six different beers in the past year alone.

Beardsell's original business plan included selling his beer in kegs to other restaurants and pubs, but instead he has been forced to work hard just to keep up with demand at the Pig. Based on how busy the pub was on the Sunday evening I was there and the restaurant manager's anecdotes about beer geeks lining up with growlers outside the door when special beers are scheduled to go on tap, Kamloops has clearly become a craft beer hot spot. Most of the beer I tasted was excellent, as was the meal I enjoyed sitting outside on the sun-dappled patio under a spreading canopy of hops—which they would pick to use in a special batch of beer in a few weeks' time.

If I lived in Kamloops, the Pig would be my second home. I'll have to satisfy myself with planning regular trips there so I can enjoy these noble brews.

Facts & Figures

OPENED ‣ *2010* ✪ **STYLES PRODUCED** ‣ *6 + numerous seasonals* ✪ **WHERE TO BUY** ‣ *At the brewpub* ✪ **GROWLERS** ‣ *Yes*

Ridge Brewpub

|||||||||||||||||||||||||||||||||||||||||||||

Tap List

RGD
5% ABV
An unfortunately bland imitation of the popular "genuine draft" macro beer style.

RIDGE HONEY ALE
5% ABV
The addition of honey gives this blonde ale a bit of flavour, but not much.

IF YOU LIKE summertime heat, Osoyoos is the place to go in B.C. It is often the hottest place in Canada, with daily average temperatures of over 30°c in July and August. Osoyoos Lake is the perfect place to beat the heat—its waters are among the warmest in B.C. each summer. The near-desert landscape is gorgeous.

However, if you want to cool off with a chilled craft beer, you better bring your own or visit the local liquor store. The only brewpub in the area, which is part of the West Ridge resort located on the western edge of town, is not worth visiting. On the evening I stopped in, near the end of summer, the bartender seemed surprised when I asked for a set of samplers of their beer, and judging by the big-brewery lagers lining the shelves of the big fridges behind the bar, I doubt if many customers make the same request.

Facts & Figures

OPENED ▸ *1999* ✪ **STYLES PRODUCED ▸** *5* ✪ **ON TAP ▸** *The brewpub* ✪ **GROWLERS ▸** *No*

Tin Whistle Brewing

250-770-1122
954 Eckhardt Avenue W.,
Penticton

THE FIRST BREWERY to open in the Okanagan in 1995, Tin Whistle was purchased by Lorraine Nagy in 1998 as a retirement project even though she didn't know much about beer—she thought she'd build it up it for five years before selling it and retiring for good. Fifteen years later, she is still at the helm. She says that since 2006 the brewery has seen a 400 per cent increase in sales, one of the biggest success stories in B.C.'s craft beer boom.

It's a small operation, struggling to brew enough beer to keep up with demand, and up until recently brewer Jeff Tod was not allowed much leeway in creating new brews. Early in 2012, however, Nagy finally acquiesced to his requests to brew an IPA. Not wanting to squander the opportunity, he jumped into the deep end with a very bold 8 per cent brew called Scorpion Double IPA.

It will be interesting to see what the future holds; in the right hands, I think Tin Whistle could really capitalize on its established brand and get out from under the shadow of Cannery and Tree.

Tap List

**KILLER BEE
DARK HONEY ALE**

6% ABV

A tasty dark brew that combines roasted malt flavours with the smooth sweetness of honey.

SCORPION DOUBLE IPA

8% ABV | 75 IBU

A big, malty IPA with a dash of citrusy West Coast hops.

Facts & Figures

OPENED › *1995* ✪ **STYLES PRODUCED ›** *6* ✪ **WHERE TO BUY ›** *At the brewery and at liquor stores throughout B.C.* ✪ **ON TAP ›** *Restaurants and bars in Penticton* ✪ **GROWLERS ›** *Yes*

www.treebeer.com
250-717-1091
1083 Richter Street, Kelowna
E-MAIL info@treebeer.com
TWITTER @TreeBrewing

Tree Brewing

IIIIIIIIIIIIIIIIIIIIIIIIIIIIIIIIIIIIIIIIIIIII

I FIRST VISITED Tree Brewing in the mid-1990s when my high school buddy, Ken Belau, became the first brewer there after graduating from a brewing university in Germany. I loved touring the facility and tasting fresh beer right at the source. In retrospect, I see now that it was one of the early experiences that pushed me down the road to writing this guidebook. Having such a personal connection to the beer meant a lot to me and got me more excited about searching out other beers and learning about the people and places behind them.

The brewery went through a few ownership changes in its early years and Ken moved on to other jobs in other places. I only managed one trip out to Kelowna while he was working there, but I've always kept an eye on the place. When it stabilized in the past decade I was happy to report the news to Ken. That success and stability had a lot to with the skills of brewmaster Stefan Buhl, who applied his distinctly German work ethic to the place.

As he explains while touring the brewery, "We don't make anything sweet. We ferment it properly." Similarly, he frowns at the idea of experimentation or guesswork in brewing.

Tap List

THIRSTY BEAVER AMBER ALE

5% ABV

Available in both six-packs and a budget-price single tall can, this is a medium-bodied amber ale.

HOP HEAD IPA

5.6% ABV | 65 IBU

One of the earliest IPAS in B.C. to feature West Coast hops prominently, Hop Head is still solid although it has been surpassed by other hoppier IPAS.

MADCAP BELGIAN WHITE ALE

5% ABV

A tasty Belgian wit—ideal for summer patio season.

CAPTIVATOR DOPPELBOCK

8% ABV

This rich, malty Doppelbock is a style not commonly brewed in B.C.—and rarely this well.

The way he sees it, there is one way to brew beer: "The right way."

Buhl's philosophy shows through in the quality of the beers he produces. His Pilsner is the only German style in the regular lineup of beers, not surprising given the more British origins of craft beer in B.C. Tree does produce a wide range of rather un-German ales, including the potent Hop Head IPA which was one of the earliest examples of a true West Coast IPA in B.C. And they recently added some bigger hop bombs to the Hop Head lineup: a delicious Double IPA (8.3 per cent ABV, 90 IBU) and an exceptional Black IPA (8.8 per cent ABV, 61 IBU).

Tree is now the Okanagan's largest brewery, and one of the province's major players in the craft brewing scene. They sell a diverse lineup of beer styles in a variety of packages, including six-packs of bottles and cans, single 500 mL cans, bombers for the specialty beers, and mixed twelve-packs of bottles. In addition to the hop bombs, Tree also produces several seasonals, including a pumpkin beer, the popular Vertical Winter Ale, Madcap Belgian White Ale, and two authentic German beers—a Hefeweizen and Captivator Doppelbock— where Buhl's origins truly shine.

Facts & Figures

OPENED ▸ *1996* ✪ **STYLES PRODUCED** ▸ *5 + 5 seasonals* ✪ **WHERE TO BUY** ▸ *At the brewery and liquor stores throughout B.C.* ✪ **ON TAP** ▸ *Throughout the Okanagan* ✪ **GROWLERS** ▸ *Only Tree "braulers" (stainless steel growlers that sell for about $45)*

BEST BEERS

Thompson-Okanagan

. . . .

Naramata Nut Brown Ale
Cannery's original beer and still one of the best in the region: a creamy, malty brown ale.

Crannóg Ales Gael's Blood Potato Ale
About as Irish as you can get coming from an Irish Farmhouse brewery in the heart of B.C.

Firehall Brewery Holy Smoke Stout
A blend of Rauchbier (smoked beer) and stout: this is a unique and special beer.

Noble Pig Brewhouse Empress of India Imperial Rye IPA
A potent brew with a depth of malt and hop flavours that has me planning annual trips to Kamloops around its brew schedule.

Tree Brewing Hop Head Black India Pale Ale
Call it a Cascadian Dark Ale or a Black IPA: either way, this is a rich, dark beer with a great roasted malt character and a big bite of hops.

THE
★ KOOTENAYS ★

AT THE BREWERY	DRAFT	FOOD	GROWLERS	BOTTLE SALES	TOURS	BEDS
Arrowhead Brewing			✪		✪	
Fernie Brewing			✪	✪	✪	
Mt. Begbie Brewing				✪	✪	
Nelson Brewing				✪	✪	

MOUNTAINS
OF BEER

....

ALTHOUGH I HAVE driven across B.C. many times over the past two decades I never really took much time to explore the Kootenays region since I was usually in a rush to get somewhere else. When I finally made it there on my Craft Beer Odyssey I wished I had slowed down to explore the area long ago. I loved the incredible natural scenery, of course, but more than that I enjoyed getting to know some of the communities and the people involved in the beer industry there. The common refrain I heard from the craft breweries I visited in Revelstoke, Fernie and Nelson was that before they opened there was virtually no interesting beer in the marketplace there. Everyone was drinking Bud or Kokanee. And even when these small breweries took the risk and launched themselves, it was a long, uphill struggle to get noticed and gain acceptance.

But the shared conclusions to their stories is that their hard work paid off and now Mt. Begbie Brewing, Fernie Brewing and Nelson Brewing are all successful enterprises that have earned respect and support, not only in their own towns, but also in the surrounding area, and even across the provincial border in Alberta. This sort of happy ending must be inspiring to a new start-up like Arrowhead Brewing in Invermere, which hopes to emulate its neighbours' business models.

This section was actually called "The Kootenays and the North" when I began writing this book, but, unfortunately, I had to delete B.C.'s only northern craft brewery just before going to press. Smithers' Plan B Brewing, the most remote brewery in B.C., which was founded in 2008, closed early in 2013. A nanobrewery, owner Mark Gillis was faced with the dilemma of either closing or expanding to make it more viable. A father with three young children, he chose to close the business rather than spend any more sixty-hour weeks away from his family. Hopefully, breweries planned for nearby Terrace and Prince Rupert will be able to pick up the craft brewing torch in northern B.C.

Arrowhead Brewing

|||||||||||||||||||||||||||||||||||||||||

Tap List

**BLONDE
BOMBSHELL ALE**

5% ABV

Light and refreshing but with far more depth and flavour than you might expect.

DRY IRISH STOUT

5% ABV

A rich, satisfying stout in the best Irish tradition.

THIS IS ONE of the newest breweries included in this book, but as far as co-founder Shawn Tegart is concerned, it's been in the works for fifteen years. That's when he returned to B.C. after a stint living in Oregon and found himself missing the quality and range of craft beer he'd enjoyed there. He homebrewed for a time, then finally made the leap to this full-scale operation with his wife, Leanne, as his partner.

Arrowhead's brand is styled after classic mid-twentieth century designs, a theme the brewery plans to embrace by hosting vintage car shows and burlesque nights. The Tegarts think they will need to spend some time educating local consumers about craft beer styles, but they are also counting on a lot of interest from international tourists visiting the local ski hill and hot springs.

Facts & Figures

OPENED ‣ *2012* ✪ **STYLES PRODUCED** ‣ *4 + limited releases* ✪ **WHERE TO BUY** ‣ *The brewery* ✪ **ON TAP** ‣ *Throughout the Invermere area* ✪ **GROWLERS** ‣ *Yes*

EAST KOOTENAY
BEER FESTIVAL

. . . .

Held on a weekend in mid-June each year

A WELCOME addition to the beer festival scene in B.C., this event was held for the first time in 2012. Interest in craft beer is growing steadily in the East Kootenays, thanks especially to the efforts of companies like Mt. Begbie Brewing, Fernie Brewing and Nelson Brewing, as well the newest kid on the block in nearby Invermere, Arrowhead Brewing. More than fifty beers from sixteen breweries from B.C., Alberta and Yukon were showcased in the inaugural event. While this festival includes a few brands that might not be considered "craft beer," it is definitely a positive step in the right direction.

The Fairmont Hot Springs Resort, which hosts this event, is a comfortable year-round destination with rejuvenating, odourless hot spring pools, restaurants, golf courses and many other outdoor activities.

www.fairmonthotsprings.com

www.ferniebrewing.com
250-423-7797
26 Manitou Road, Fernie
E-MAIL abi@ferniebrewing.com
TWITTER @ferniebrewingco

Fernie Brewing

||||||||||||||||||||||||||||||||||||||||

Tap List

**FIRST TRAX
BROWN ALE**
5% ABV
Chocolaty and nutty
thanks to a blend of eight
specialty malts.

OL' WILLY WIT
5% ABV
A seasonal beer that is now
produced year-round due
to popularity, this Belgian
wit is brewed with coriander and curacao orange
peel.

**WHAT THE HUCK
HUCKLEBERRY WHEAT**
5% ABV
A B.C. original: the huckleberry is native to the Rocky
Mountain region. It works
well in this purple-tinged
wheat beer.

**PUMPKIN HEAD
BROWN ALE** (seasonal)
5% ABV | 17 IBU
One of the best pumpkin
beers in B.C., this brown
ale has a rich, roasted malt
character that blends perfectly with the pumpkin.

WHEN FERNIE BREWING first opened in 2003,
it was one of those rarest of breweries that
was actually busier in the winter than in the
summer. That's because during ski season,
there were generally more people (about nine
thousand) on the slopes of the three ski hills
situated around the town of Fernie than
actually lived there year-round (about five
thousand). That meant the bars and restaurants on the slopes and the après-ski spots in
town were packed whenever there was fresh
powder. And since many of those skiers were
coming from elsewhere, especially places
like Europe, they were often more interested
in craft beer styles than boring mass-market
North American lagers.

That gave Fernie Brewing a good start in
the business, but over the decade since then,
the traditional brewer's model of just trying
to keep up with the insatiable demand during the summer has definitely taken over,
especially following the brewery's move from
its original facility in a farm shed to its current setup just off Highway 3 in 2007.

While the small town of Fernie itself
could not sustainably support a mid-sized
craft brewery, the company has done a great
job of finding other markets for its products.

Being so close to the Alberta border, the brewery enjoys a lot of popularity in the Calgary area, and its excellent, diverse range of beers is also available throughout B.C. in government liquor stores. They are one of a handful of B.C. breweries that offer a mixed sampler pack—both a summer and winter seasonal version. It's a great concept that responds to the craft beer consumer's innate desire for variety.

Fernie has also responded to the howls of consumer demand by adding the Lone Wolf IPA to its lineup, along with a series of seasonal beers in 650 mL bomber bottles that definitely are directed at the craft beer drinker's palate: Ol' Willy Wit, Pumpkin Head Brown Ale, What the Huck Huckleberry Wheat, and Sap Sucker Maple Porter.

As with the other Kootenay breweries I visited on my Craft Beer Odyssey, Fernie's pubs and restaurants definitely support the local brewery by selling a range of their products. But I also noticed a strong interest in other craft beer there, including brands from south of the border, which is very positive. It's not about creating competition for the brewery, but rather encouraging consumers to develop their interest in craft beer styles, and creating lifelong craft beer drinkers.

When you visit Fernie, be sure to ask a local about the legend of the Ghostrider. It's a great spooky story to enjoy over a pint of beer.

Facts & Figures

OPENED › 2003 ✿ **STYLES PRODUCED ›** 6 + 3 seasonals
✿ **WHERE TO BUY ›** Liquor stores throughout B.C. ✿
ON TAP › Throughout the East Kootenays and in select places in the Okanagan and Greater Vancouver ✿ **GROWLERS ›** Yes

www.mt-begbie.com
250-837-2756
521 First Street West, Revelstoke
E-MAIL tlarson@mtbegbie.com

Mt. Begbie Brewing

||||||||||||||||||||||||||||||||||||||||||||

HOW MANY BREWERIES do you know that are run by a nuclear physicist?

There is probably only one: Mt. Begbie Brewing, where the founding brewer, Bart Larson, has a PhD in nuclear physics. His wife and business partner, Tracey, is no academic slouch either, with a background in zoology and biology. So how did they end up running a brewery in Revelstoke? Love, of course: for each other and for beer. Tracey says it was a honeymoon conversation: "Hey, maybe we should start a brewery." And even though neither of them had any experience brewing beer, they knew people involved with the original Shaftebury brewery in Vancouver, and the dream grew and grew until they found themselves setting up shop in Bart's hometown of Revelstoke.

Tracey remembers arriving there on New Year's Eve after there had been a huge dump of snow and wondering, "What have I gotten myself into?" But then she felt so welcomed by neighbours who invited them over for a New Year's hot tub party that she knew it was the right decision.

Initially, Bart and Tracey were the brewery's sole employees. Bart focused on the brewing while Tracey handled

Tap List

HIGH COUNTRY KOLSCH
4.5% ABV
An excellent Kölsch: a light, mildly hopped wheat ale.

BOB'S YOUR DUNKEL
8% ABV
A rich Dunkelweizen: sweet and malty with roasted barley and chocolate flavours.

NASTY HABIT IPA
6% ABV
A very popular English IPA with a good bitterness and solid malt backbone.

ATILLA THE HONEY (seasonal)
5% ABV
An amber ale with the distinctive taste of clover honey.

administration and marketing, as well as all the deliveries, including innumerable drives across Rogers Pass during the brutal winters the region is famous for. At first, they thought they could just focus on selling their beer in Revelstoke, but they quickly realized they had to expand beyond the small city's borders to sustain the business.

And expand is exactly what they have done. Mt. Begbie Brewing now has three brewers on staff; Bart mainly oversees things, but he keeps busy fixing and automating the brewing systems himself. Tracey runs the administrative side, and says she doesn't miss delivering the beer, although she "probably could still drive the forklift."

Mt. Begbie Brewing has worked hard to build a customer base in the Revelstoke area. When they started, everyone seemed to drink Bud and Kokanee, and Tracey says it took a while, but suddenly in the last few years, it's become easier. She thinks it might have to do with the new ski hill that opened there a few years ago, since it attracts out-of-town visitors and seasonal employees who might already be used to more complex and challenging styles. It says something that their Nasty Habit IPA is now their biggest seller in bottles, when, according to Tracey, "six years ago that wouldn't have been possible." It was wonderful to see local restaurants proudly pouring their beers, especially an unusual and complex seasonal such as Hillaswilla Wit, which was on tap all over town.

....
Facts & Figures

OPENED ‣ *1996* ✪ **STYLES PRODUCED** ‣ *5 + 2 seasonals* ✪ **WHERE TO BUY** ‣ *Liquor stores throughout B.C.* ✪ **ON TAP** ‣ *Throughout the Revelstoke area and select places in the Okanagan and Greater Vancouver* ✪ **GROWLERS** ‣ *No*

www.nelsonbrewing.com
250-352-3582
512 Latimer Street, Nelson
E-MAIL nbc@netidea.com

Nelson Brewing

Tap List

HARVEST MOON ORGANIC HEMP ALE

4.2% ABV

This Kölsch-style ale is as close as you'll get to a lager from Nelson Brewing, and the toasted hemp seeds add a little something-something.

NELSON AFTER DARK

5% ABV

A British-style Dark Mild ale, this is delicious and surprisingly quaffable despite its dark colour. "Everyone looks better after dark."

PADDYWHACK IPA

6.5% ABV

One of the great original B.C. IPAs, Paddywhack is still one of the tastiest and most well-balanced around.

FACEPLANT WINTER ALE (seasonal)

6.5% ABV

This might be my favourite B.C. winter seasonal beer. No mulling spices or vanilla, but some great body and flavour from added molasses and brown sugar.

AFTER I MOVED to B.C. from Ontario in 1991, Nelson soon reached the top of my list of places I wanted to visit here. Everything I heard about this West Kootenay community made it sound better and better: fine heritage architecture (with some buildings designed by Francis Rattenbury, the same architect who was responsible for the provincial legislature and the Empress Hotel in Victoria); many artists and craftspeople; a strong focus on local and organic food production; the hippie, draft dodger culture that helped drive its revitalization in the 1970s and '80s; and the beer, of course. I finally made it to Nelson as part of my Craft Beer Odyssey road trip and I can't believe I waited twenty-one years to do so. Maybe it was my ponytail-length hair, but everywhere I went I felt so comfortable and welcome.

But what about the beer? Nelson has a brewing history that goes back to 1897 and includes a spell as home to one of the Columbia Brewing chain of breweries. That all ended by the 1960s, but then the contemporary incarnation of Nelson Brewing opened in 1991 in the same building that housed the original Columbia brewery. The company has evolved considerably over its two decades plus, but the biggest transition occurred in 2006 when it decided to go all-organic, reflecting the healthy, organic life-style embraced by many Nelsonites.

The organic focus severely limits the choice of ingredients available to the brewery. Hops, especially, can be hard to get since certain varieties of the trendy, newer West Coast styles are simply not available from organic farms. Happily, that situation is changing with the growth of organic hops production in the U.S. and Canada, as well as abroad. Perhaps surprisingly, no hops are produced locally in Nelson, although it might have something to do with another significant local crop taking priority (wink wink, nudge nudge).

Nelson Brewing has just finished making some big changes to its lineup: adding a 473 mL tall can, moving some of its other core brands into 355 mL cans, and beginning a series of specialty brews in 650 mL bombers. While most, if not all, of their beer is available throughout B.C., don't wait twenty-one years to visit this vibrant community in person. Go to the source. Maybe I'll see you there.

Facts & Figures

OPENED › *1991* ✪ **STYLES PRODUCED ›** *6 + seasonals and limited releases* ✪ **WHERE TO BUY ›** *Liquor stores throughout B.C.* ✪ **ON TAP ›** *Throughout the Kootenays and at select places in the Okanagan and Greater Vancouver.* ✪ **GROWLERS ›** *No*

THE LION'S HEAD

An oasis of
craft beer in Bud country

······················

IN ROBSON, just across the Columbia River from Castlegar, about forty-five minutes west of Nelson, the Lion's Head Smoke and Brew Pub is an oasis of craft beer in the West Kootenay region. They do not brew their own beer, but instead offer twelve craft taps featuring a cross-section of great beer from all across the province. This is "Bud country," a lesson the owners, Troy Pyett and Carly Hadfield, learned the hard way when they opened in June 2009. Carly, daughter of Spinnakers' publican Paul Hadfield, says they sold out of their small stock of Budweiser bottles in the first hour without selling any of the craft beer they had on tap.

"It was touch and go at first," she admits. "People thought we were crazy." They even faced a boycott from the local community who wanted them to drop the craft beer entirely. But they stuck to their cheeky motto: "Converting Bud drinkers and vegetarians since 2009," and it has paid off. "People began coming out of the woodwork," Carly says. Now, the place is busy all the time. They have added outdoor patio sections, hold an Oktoberfest pig roast each fall, and have live music as well. The pub has an excellent menu, featuring a variety of meats that are smoked right on site. I can vouch for the incredible brisket sandwich.

Their dozen taps usually feature six Spinnakers brews along with rotating taps from local breweries such as Tree Brewing, Nelson Brewing, Fernie Brewing, Mt. Begbie Brewing, Crannóg Ales and Cannery Brewing. It was great to get a taste of home, in my case a Spinnakers Northwest Ale, which became one of my favourite beers after I moved back to Victoria in 2012.

Carly and Troy believe it is important to educate their customers about craft beer, so they offer sampler racks, and the chalkboard list of brews on tap includes descriptions of the beers. Troy also co-hosts a local radio show every Friday afternoon where he talks about craft beer.

Carly says the sold-out cask festival they held three years to the day they took possession of the pub was her proudest moment. And on a daily basis, it's incredible to see the variety of beer people are drinking there: "Just to walk around and see six different colours of beer on one table."

www.lionsheadpub.ca
250-365-BREW (2739)
2629 Broadwater Road
Robson
TWITTER @lionsheadpubbc

BEST BEERS

The Kootenays
& Northern B.C.

....

Fernie Brewing What the Huck
A standout among B.C. berry beers, this huckleberry-infused wheat ale is a delicious year-round brew.

Fernie Brewing Sap Sucker Maple Porter
The addition of maple syrup gives this beer a unique edge among B.C. porters.

Mt. Begbie Brewing Nasty Habit IPA
A big seller in the Kootenays, this delicious IPA is available throughout B.C. and is worth checking out.

Nelson Brewing Full Nelson Imperial IPA
Brewed with Nelson Sauvin hops from New Zealand, so-named because they smell distinctly of Cabernet Sauvignon grapes, this IPA has a unique aroma and flavour.

Nelson Brewing Paddywhack IPA
A long-time standard of the IPA style in B.C., you can't go wrong with this organic beer.

8

CAPS
CORKS
&
COASTERS

★ ★

B.C.'S CRAFT BEER
HISTORY & FUTURE

....

1982

› Horseshoe Bay Brewing starts brewing beer for the Troller Pub, kick-starting B.C.'s Craft Beer Revolution.

1984

› Spinnakers, Canada's first true brewpub, opens in Victoria.
› Canada's first microbrewery, Granville Island Brewing, opens in Vancouver.
› Island Pacific Brewing opens in Victoria. It changes its name to Vancouver Island Brewery in 1989.

1985

› CAMRA B.C. launches in Victoria, and Okanagan Spring Brewery opens in Vernon.

1987

› Shaftebury Brewing opens in Vancouver.

1989

› Swans Brewpub/Buckerfields Brewery opens in Victoria with some help from craft beer godfather Frank Appleton.

1991

> Nelson Brewing opens. Fifteen years later, it goes all organic.
> Whistler Brewing opens.

1993

> Great Canadian Beer Festival begins in Victoria. Although it starts small, it is now B.C.'s biggest and most important annual beer festival.

1994

> Bowen Island Brewing opens.
> Sailor Hagar's begins brewing its own beer. Its brewmaster, Gary Lohin, would later open craft beer powerhouse Central City Brewing.
> Storm Brewing opens in Vancouver.
> Tall Ship Ale Company opens in Squamish.
> Yaletown Brewing, Vancouver's first brewpub, opens.

1995

> Bastion City Brewing opens in Nanaimo, but closes its doors two years later.
> Bear Brewing opens in Kamloops. Six years later it acquires the Whistler and Bowen Island brands, then sells to Big Rock Brewing in 2003.
> Okanagan Fest-of-Ale launches in Penticton.
> Russell Brewing opens in Surrey.
> Steamworks Brew Pub opens in Vancouver.
> Tin Whistle Brewing opens in Penticton.

1996

> Canoe Brewpub opens in Victoria.
> Hopscotch Festival launches in Vancouver.
> Howe Sound Brewing and Inn opens with the help of John Mitchell, one half of the original Horseshoe Bay Brewing team.
> Mission Springs Brewing opens in Mission.

- Mt. Begbie Brewing opens in Revelstoke.
- Tree Brewing opens in Kelowna with my buddy Ken Belau as its first brewmaster.

1997

- BrewHouse High Mountain Brewing opens in Whistler.
- Big River Brewpub opens in Richmond.
- Dockside Brewing and R&B Brewing open in Vancouver.
- Wild Horse Brewing opens in Penticton and Windermere Brewing opens in Invermere, but each brews for only two years before closing its doors. Kimberley Brewing opens, but closes a year later.

1998

- Autumn Brewmasters' Festival launches in Vancouver and runs annually until 2006.
- Backwoods Brewing opens in Aldergrove. Eight years later it changes its name to Dead Frog Brewery.
- Dix BBQ & Brewery opens in Vancouver and operates for twelve years before closing its doors.
- Gulf Islands Brewery opens on Salt Spring Island. In 2011, it rebrands as Salt Spring Island Ales.
- Lighthouse Brewing opens in Victoria.

1999

- Big Ridge Brewing opens in Surrey and Longwood Brewpub opens in Nanaimo.

2000

- Crannóg Ales, the first certified organic brewery in Canada, opens in Sorrento.
- Fat Cat Brewery opens in Nanaimo. Eleven years later, it changes ownership, becoming Wolf Brewing.
- Old Yale Brewing opens in Chilliwack.

2001

> Cannery Brewing opens in Penticton.
> Freddy's Brewpub opens in Kelowna.
> Phillips Brewing opens in Victoria.

2003

> Central City Brewing opens in Surrey and Fernie Brewing opens.

2004

> Avalon Brewing opens in North Vancouver, and later becomes Taylor's Crossing Restaurant & Brewery. Unfortunately, it closes in 2011.

2005

> The Mark James Group—owners of Taylor's Crossing, Yaletown Brewing, Surrey's Big Ridge and Whistler's BrewHouse—begin brewing Red Truck beer.

2006

> Barley Station Brew Pub opens in Salmon Arm.
> Canada Cup of Beer launches in Vancouver.
> Craig Street Brewpub opens in Duncan.

2008

> Plan B Brewing opens in Smithers, brewing for five years before closing in 2013.
> Surgenor Brewing opens in Comox, but closes three year later.
> Driftwood Brewery opens in Victoria.

2010

> Noble Pig Brewhouse opens in Kamloops.
> Vancouver Craft Beer Week is launched.

2011

> Barley's Angels—Pink Pints Chapter, B.C.'s first women's beer group, and B.C. Craft Beer Month are launched.
> Hoyne Brewing and Moon Under Water Brew Pub open in Victoria.
> Tofino Brewing opens in Tofino.

2012

- Arrowhead Brewing opens in Invermere.
- Bridge Brewing opens in North Vancouver.
- Coal Harbour Brewing, Parallel 49 Brewing and Powell Street Craft Brewery open within a few blocks of each other in East Vancouver.
- East Kootenay Beer Festival launches in Fairmont Hot Springs.
- Firehall Brewery opens in Oliver.
- Townsite Brewing opens in Powell River.

2013

- Four Winds Brewing opens in Delta.
- The HeidOut Brewhouse opens in Cranbrook.
- 33 Acres Brewing opens in Vancouver.
- Deep Cove Brewers and Distillers opens in North Vancouver.

JUST AROUND
THE CORNER

New craft breweries
in the works in B.C.

••••••••••••••••••••••

THE FUTURE looks bright for craft beer in British Columbia with several new breweries in the planning stages and many more rumoured to be opening soon.

The biggest developments are new production breweries for Central City Brewing, Red Truck Beer and Steamworks Brewing, all of which should open in 2013. This will increase those breweries' capacity considerably, allowing them to answer demand for their current beers and giving them a chance to add new styles to their rosters. It could also mean more great B.C. beer gets shipped out of the province—east to the prairies and Ontario and south to thirsty markets in the U.S. I am fine with that as long as they keep making it for us here; exporting it out of province is a great way to showcase just how good we have it.

Three other brewpubs—Longwood, Mission Springs and Spinnakers—all have plans to open separate production facilities, which will allow them to package and sell their beers beyond what their current capacities allow.

In addition to Brassneck Brewery and Main Street Brewing, at least five other new breweries are planned for the Vancouver area: 33 Acres Brewing; Bomber Brewing (which is connected to the Biercraft chain); Dogwood Brewing with Claire Connolly (previously the brewer at Big River Brewpub) as brewmaster; Four Winds Brewing (in Delta); and Sapperton Brewing (in New Westminster). The aptly named Beachcomber Brewery is planned for Gibsons on the lower Sunshine Coast, and Deep Cove Brewing & Distilling plans to open in North Vancouver. I have also heard rumours of new breweries in Duncan, North Vancouver, and the West Shore area of Greater Victoria, but nothing has been confirmed. Plans to build a new brewpub in the Cambie Hotel building have apparently been scuttled because of Gastown development regulations.

The Four Mile Pub in View Royal, just outside Victoria, is planning to convert into a brewpub by the fall of 2013. I am sure that Victoria will see even more growth, especially in the surrounding suburbs. Certainly, the West Shore (Langford/Colwood) could easily support another brewpub and a micro-brewery or two. Places like Sidney and Brentwood Bay on the Saanich peninsula seem ripe for brewpubs.

What is especially exciting to me is to see new breweries planned for relatively remote regions: Wheelhouse Brewing intends to open in Prince Rupert in 2013 and Skeena Brewing hopes to open in Terrace in 2014. As well, the Noble Pig's owner, David Beardsell, has a new brewpub in the works in Cranbrook—a welcome addition to the Kootenay region, which really seems to be waking up to craft beer.

I would love to see more breweries or brewpubs in other smaller communities, such as Courtenay, Campbell River, Castlegar, Hope, Kimberley and Creston (watch out, Kokanee!). And it would be great to see more brewpubs on the Gulf Islands. I also think there is potential for growth in some markets where there is only one craft beer option right now, such as Kamloops, Kelowna and Richmond. Prince George also needs some craft beer, although maybe the locals see Pacific Western in that light, even if I don't.

Hopefully, when it comes down to revising this book for its tenth anniversary edition (take note, dear publisher), it will be a much expanded version with new breweries in every region. I'm confident it will be.

YOU'RE
SOAKING IN IT

Why some so-called
craft breweries don't make the cut
to be included in this book
and one owned by Molson does

•••••••••••••••••••••••

As I was researching and writing this book, I had to make some difficult decisions about whether or not certain breweries qualified as "craft breweries." In some cases, it was easy: obviously, the so-called "macrobreweries," the big national brands, Molson and Labatt, don't count as craft breweries, and neither do their imitation craft lines, Rickard's and Alexander Keith's. Astute readers will note, however, that I did include Granville Island Brewing, which was purchased in 2009 by Molson-Coors through their Ontario micro brand, Creemore Springs. Molson seems to have been fairly hands-off with GIB, and I consider the specialty beers brewed by Vern Lambourne in the original brewhouse on Granville Island to be craft beer for sure. So Granville Island makes the cut.

One step down from those breweries is a level often described as "regional breweries." This includes some breweries that started as microbreweries but then grew into larger entities that eventually got swallowed up by bigger breweries. Okanagan Spring Brewery is the best example of that in B.C. In order to achieve a certain size, regional breweries like OK Spring often end up sacrificing the quality of their ingredients and pulling back on flavours in order to make them more palatable to a wider audience. Well, that ain't craft.

Likewise, I did not include the Turning Point Brewery, makers of Stanley Park Amber and Pilsner. I dislike this brewery for so many reasons. First, there is its spurious claim that its single wind turbine somehow generates enough power to run the whole "sustainable" brewery. Second is use of the "Stanley Park Brewery, est. 1897." Turning Point has no actual connection to the public entity managed by the City of Vancouver, nor the Stanley Park Brewery, which was one of Vancouver's early breweries; its physical brewery is located on Annacis Island in Delta, nowhere near downtown Vancouver. Clearly, they are just capitalizing on the marketing value of the name.

Turning Point is owned by the Mark Anthony Group, a large alcohol distributor based in Kelowna and connected with the Mission Hill Winery. When the company lost the rights to distribute Corona, owner Anthony van Mandl built his own brewery. That's why Stanley Park beer showed up everywhere in B.C. so quickly, including in Rogers Arena and BC Place Stadium, where no craft beer has ever been sold yet. It's all about marketing and connections, baby—but definitely not about the beer.

Speaking of the actual beer, Turning Point claims its "1897 Amber is a Belgian style Amber, regarded by brewers to be the most complex and distinctive, but also the most difficult to craft." That's all hogwash. What they brew certainly isn't distinctive or difficult to make. Taste it next to any real Belgian beer and you will certainly notice the difference. The brewery also produces Hell's Gate lager and pale ale, which might best be described as "gateway beers," aimed at bridging the gap between traditional Kokanee, Lucky or Bud drinkers. In other words, Turning Point is closer to being a marketing company that brews beer than an actual craft brewery.

Here are some other breweries that didn't make the cut:
Pacific Western is a large, independent brewery based in Prince George that sometimes brews beer that craft beer drinkers might enjoy. I've happily sipped their Canterbury Dark Mild,

a brand that goes way back in B.C., or their Pacific Schwarzbock, on occasion, and they have an organic line called NatureLand that features a lager and an amber ale. They also brew the Cariboo line, which is an entry-level lineup. In the end, it comes down to my interpretation of "craft beer" (see "What is Craft Beer Anyway?" on page 4): although independent, PW's focus isn't on brewing high-quality beer across the board. Close, though.

Including Whistler Brewing is this book was debatable. If they didn't have an actual brewery in Whistler, I probably wouldn't have done so. The brewery's parent company, NorthAm Group, also produces the Bowen Island brand of budget craft imitators and, occasionally, Black Bear Ale, once a Bear Brewing brand. Although both Bowen Island and Bear have places in the history of craft brewing in B.C., I didn't include them because they are not independent operations.

Shaftebury has a great history in B.C., but its brand was bought by Okanagan Spring in 1999 and now it is sold as a budget craft brand, similar to Bowen Island. It doesn't make the cut, although if Shaftebury Cream Ale is the only thing in the cooler at a barbecue, I certainly won't turn it down.

FURTHER
TASTING

• •

AWARD-WINNING BREWS
Here are some of the B.C. craft breweries and individual beers
that won awards in 2012.

Canadian Brewing Awards—2012 (B.C. breweries won 40 per cent
of the awards!)

Canadian Brewery of the Year—Central City Brewing

Gold Medals
Vancouver Islander Lager, Vancouver Island Brewery
Hermann's Dark Lager, Vancouver Island Brewery
Coffee Porter, R&B Brewing
Red Racer ESB, Central City Brewing
Swans Scotch Ale, Swans Brewpub
Nagila Pale Ale, Yaletown Brewing
Steamworks Pale Ale, Steamworks Brewing
Sungod Wheat Ale, R&B Brewing
Woolly Bugger barley wine, Howe Sound Brewing
Powell IPA, Coal Harbour Brewing
Central City Imperial IPA, Central City Brewing
Mandarin Orange Amber Ale, Dead Frog Brewery

Dark Snout Bacon Stout, R&B Brewing
Thor's Hammer Bourbon Barrel Barley Wine,
     Central City Brewing

B.C. Beer Awards—2012
Best of Show—Steamworks Pilsner—Conrad Gmoser of
Steamworks Brewing

Category Winners
Steamworks Pilsner—Steamworks Brewing
High Country Kölsch—Mt. Begbie Brewing
Belgian White—Lighthouse Brewing
Red Racer Pale Ale—Central City Brewing
Skookum Cascadian Brown Ale—Phillips Brewing
Pow Town Porter—Townsite Brewing
Big Caboose Red Ale—Fernie Brewing
Blackberry Festivale—Townsite Brewing
Keepers Stout—Lighthouse Brewing
5 Rings IPA—BrewHouse High Mountain
     Brewing
Oud Bruin—Yaletown Brewing
Smoke & Mirrors Imperial Smoked Ale—Coal Harbour
     Brewing
Hermannator Ice Bock—Vancouver Island Brewery

CAMRA Vancouver Awards—2012
Best Local Brewpub—Central City Brewing
Best B.C. Brewpub—Central City Brewing
Best B.C. Brewery (non-brewpub)—Driftwood Brewery
Best B.C. Beer—Driftwood Brewery Fat Tug IPA
Best B.C. Seasonal Beer—Driftwood Brewery Sartori
     Harvest IPA

HOPHEADS
UNITE

B.C.'s Biggest Hop Bombs

· ·

BACK IN the Jazz Age, the term "hophead" referred to a drug user, but these days it is used more commonly (in beer circles at least) as a slightly self-deprecating label for those who prefer hoppy styles of beer above all others, especially West Coast IPAS. You know you are a hophead when everything you buy at the bottle shop has 60-plus IBUS and a name like "Palate Wrecker." Likely, you start your night off with an 80-IBU IPA and then switch to another IPA and finish off with a third one— and can discern the different hops used in each.

For those who dedicate their taste buds to the almighty hop, I salute you. Here is a list of B.C.'s best IPAS, divided into three levels of hop explosiveness starting with the hoppiest (and ordered alphabetically to avoid arguments).

THERMONUCLEAR ICBMS
"Why is my tongue glowing in the dark?"

Central City Red Racer IPA
Central City Imperial IPA
Driftwood Fat Tug IPA
Driftwood Sartori Harvest IPA
Granville Island Imperial IPA
Howe Sound Total Eclipse of the Hop Imperial IPA

Lighthouse Switchback IPA
Phillips Amnesiac Double IPA
Swans Extra IPA
Yaletown Brick & Beam IPA

BUNKER BUSTERS
"Will my taste buds still love me in the morning?"

Bridge Deep Cove IPA
Nelson Full Nelson Imperial IPA
Parallel 49 Lord of the Hops IPA
Phillips Hop Circle IPA
Russell IP'eh!
Spinnakers Hoptoria
Storm Hurricane IPA
Tofino Hoppin' Cretin IPA
Tree Hop Head Double IPA
Whistler BrewHouse 5 Rings IPA

GRENADES
"Fire in the hole!"

Cannery IPA
Coal Harbour Powell IPA
Fernie Lone Wolf IPA
Hoyne Devil's Dream IPA
Mt. Begbie Nasty Habit IPA
Nelson Paddywhack IPA
R&B Hoppelganger IPA
Salt Spring Island Snug IPA
Townsite Tin Hat IPA
Wolf Red Brick IPA

GETTING
INVOLVED

·······················

CAMRA B.C.

THE CAMPAIGN FOR REAL ALE was founded in the UK in 1971 in response to the disappearance of traditional, cask-conditioned beer and local pub culture there. It has since grown into Britain's largest consumer group with more than 144,000 members. Over its three-plus decades, CAMRA UK has affected real positive change in the beer scene there, and hosts the Great British Beer Festival each summer.

CAMRA B.C. was first incorporated in Victoria in 1985 with similar aims: it is dedicated to the promotion and responsible consumption of natural, craft beers. It supports "the brewing of traditional styles of beer in the traditional manner, using traditional ingredients." Its mission is to act as champion of the consumer in relation to the B.C. and Canadian beer industry.

There are branches in Vancouver, Victoria and the Fraser Valley. CAMRA Vancouver's, especially, is very active: it organizes seasonal cask beer festivals and its members enjoy discounts at a wide range of private liquor stores and pubs in the city. From a political standpoint, CAMRA Vancouver's executive has been extremely vocal in recent years, campaigning for enforcement of laws that require establishments to post serving sizes (FUSS campaign) and promoting a BYOCB (bring your own craft beer) concept.

If you are interested in craft beer in B.C., I highly recommend joining CAMRA. If you live in a place without a branch, the provincial body produces a bimonthly magazine called *What's Brewing* that will help keep you informed about the beer scene here.

For more information:
www.camrabc.ca
www.camravancouver.ca
www.camrafraservalley.ca
www.camra.ca (Victoria branch)

BEER FESTIVAL CALENDAR

....

APRIL
Okanagan Fest-of-Ale (Penticton)
www.fest-of-ale.bc.ca

MAY
Vancouver Craft Beer Week
www.vancouvercraftbeerweek.com

JUNE
East Kootenay Beer Festival (Fairmont Hot Springs)
www.fairmonthotsprings.com

AUGUST
Canada Cup of Beer (Vancouver)
www.canadacupofbeer.com

SEPTEMBER
Great Canadian Beer Festival (Victoria)
www.gcbf.com

OCTOBER
B.C. Craft Beer Month
www.craftbeermonth.ca

BLOGS
& WEBSITES

. . . .

CHECK OUT these websites for more information on trends, events and news on B.C.'s craft beer scene.

Barley Mowat—A cheeky, irreverent and investigative Vancouver beer blog.
› barleymowat.com

B.C. Beer Blog—Managed by Rick Green, co-founder of Vancouver Craft Beer Week.
› bcbrews.wordpress.com

Beck's Beer Blog—Rebecca is the beer columnist for CBC Radio's "On the Coast."
› becksbeerblog.blogspot.ca

Beer on the Rock—A blog about Vancouver Island's craft beer scene by three locals.
› beerontherock.com

Brewed Awakening—Jan Zeschky blogs about beer for *The Province.*
› blogs.theprovince.com/tag/brewed-awakening/

Brewtal Truth—Victoria's Adem Tepedelen writes about beer regularly for *Decibel* magazine and will publish *Extreme Beers* in the fall of 2013.
> brewtaltruth.blogspot.ca

Daughters of Beer—Two Vancouver women who travel in search of beer.
> daughtersofbeer.tumblr.com

Green Man—Randy Shore blogs about food and beer for the *Vancouver Sun*.
> blogs.vancouversun.com/category/staff/life/food/
> the-green-man

Hop Log—Posts by Chad McCarthy: beer judge, homebrewer and world beer traveller.
> hoplogblog.blogspot.ca

Leap Beer—Chris Frederiksen reviewed one beer every day in 2012.
> leapbeer.wordpress.com

Left 4 Beer—Victoria's Ian Lloyd reviews and blogs informatively about craft beer.
> left4beer.com

Pint Sighs—Leah Poulton blogs about beer in Vancouver.
> pintsighs.blogspot.ca

Sloppy Gourmand—Blogs about beer and food by Erin Millar and Ben Coli.
> sloppygourmand.com

Urban Diner—I write a monthly "Thirsty" column and contribute beer reviews here.
> urbandiner.ca

VanEast Beer Blog—Authoritative, investigative posts by Paddy Treavor, past president of CAMRA Vancouver.

› eastsidebeer.blogspot.ca

Yet Another Damn Beer Blog—By the very funny Brendan McAleer.

› yetanotherdamnbeerblog.blogspot.ca

ACKNOWLEDGEMENTS

....

MANY PEOPLE helped me while I was researching and writing this book. I'd like to thank the tourism staff, public relations people and accommodation and restaurant partners who supported me as I travelled around B.C. conducting research in 2012. Some breweries also assisted me directly by providing accommodation and/or meals while I was visiting their communities.

And here are some shout-outs to individuals who went the extra mile:

Shawn and Jessica—for encouraging me even when I didn't believe in myself, and for providing me a home away from home so many times.

John and Nancy—for pointing out what was obvious (and for letting me win at squash once in a while, John.)

Glen—for the shared travels, the beer mug image, being my photographer—and for your photographic memory.

Enid and Linda—for your support, encouragement and interest, even though neither of you drinks beer.

Chris Labonté—for helping me take this from idea to reality.

Caroline Skelton—for jumping back into the fray and doing such a great job throughout.

The beer geeks who always have answers for my questions: Mirella Amato, Stephen Beaumont, Chester Carey, Gerry Erith, Rick Green, Paul Kamon, Crystal Luxmore, and Paddy Treavor.

SOME PARTS OF this book have appeared in slightly different form in various print and online publications. I am grateful to the publications *BCBusiness, Beer West, Northwest Brewing News, Taps, Taste, Toro, Vancouver View,* BCLiving.ca, Open-File.ca, and UrbanDiner.ca for supporting my writing and indulging my obsession with beer.

REFERENCES

••••••••••••••••••••••••

NOT ALL the research for this book was conducted on a bar stool. There are several books I consulted, all of which I encourage interested folks to seek out.

Beaumont, Stephen. *Great Canadian Beer Guide*. Toronto: Macmillan, 1994.

Coutts, Ian. *Brew North*. Vancouver: Greystone, 2010.

Morrison, Lisa M. *Craft Beers of the Pacific Northwest*. Portland: Timber Press, 2011.

Moyes, Robert. *Island Pubbing II*. Victoria: Orca, 1991.

Oliver, Garrett (ed.). *Oxford Companion to Beer*. New York: Oxford University Press, 2012.

Sneath, Allen Winn. *Brewed in Canada*. Toronto: Dundurn, 2001.

Stott, Jon. C. *Beer Quest West*. Victoria: Touchwood Editions, 2011.

OTHER SOURCES

Brewer's Gold at www.chilliwackmuseum.ca

LIST OF
BREWERIES

....

AUTHOR
NOTE

••••••••••••••••••••••

THIS BOOK was out-of-date the moment it was published, but there are lots of other ways to keep up with new brews and breweries in B.C. I write the B.C. column for the *Northwest Brewing News*, a tabloid-style newspaper that is published in Washington State and is distributed to British Columbia. I also write "Thirsty," an online column on the B.C. craft beer scene, for urbandiner.ca, where I also regularly review new and interesting beers. I tweet about beer often and will attempt to provide regular updates to the information in this book on the *Craft Beer Revolution* Facebook page and website.

Here are the links:
www.CraftBeerRevolution.ca
facebook.com/BCCraftBeerRevolution
twitter.com/CraftBeerRevolu
twitter.com/thirstywriter
thirstywriter.com
joewiebe.com

INDEX